Dream Catcher 45

Stairwell Books //

Dream Catcher 45

**Editor Emeritus
And Founder**
Paul Sutherland

Editor
Hannah Stone

Editorial Board
John Gilham (Retired Editor)
Amina Alyal (Retired Editor)
Tanya Parker Nightingale
Pauline Kirk
Rose Drew
Alan Gillott
Clint Wastling
Joe Williams
Mia Lofthouse
Caitlin Brown
Greg McGee

Art Advisor
Greg McGee

Production Managers
Alan Gillott and Rose Drew

Subscriptions to Dream Catcher Magazine

£15.00 UK (Two issues inc. p&p)
£22.00 Europe
£25.00 USA and Canada

Cheques should be made payable to **Dream Catcher** and sent to:

Dream Catcher Subscriptions

161 Lowther Street

York, YO31 7LZ

UK

+44 1904 733767

argillott@gmail.com

www.dreamcatchermagazine.co.uk
@literaryartsmag
www.stairwellbooks.co.uk
@stairwellbooks

Dream Catcher Magazine

Dream Catcher No. 45

Alan Gillott, Amina Alyal, Chris Scriven, Ciaran Buckley, Ciáran Dermott, Clifford Liles, Clint Wastling, Clive Donovan, Colette Coen, Daniel Nemo, David Harmer, David J Costello, David Sapp, Delilah Heaton, Doreen Hinchliffe, Emily Zobel Marshall, Estill Pollock, Fionola Scott, Greg McGee, Hannah Stone, Helen Heery, James B. Nicola, Jo Haslam, Joe Williams, John Gilham, Julian Matthews, Justin Lloyde, Kathleen Strafford, Kieran Furey, Lance Nizami, Mark Pearce, Martha Glaser, Martin Reed, Mary Michaels, Mia Lofthouse, Michael Henry, Michael Newman, Miriam Sulhunt, Oz Hardwick, Pat Simmons, Patrick Lodge, Pauline Kirk, Peter Datyner, Rose Drew, Simon Tindal, Stephanie Conybeare, Stephen Capus, Susie Williamson, Tanya Parker, Timothy Houghton, Tracy Dawson, Wilf Deckner,
2022

The moral rights of authors and artists have been asserted

ISSN: 1466-9455

Published by Stairwell Books //

ISBN: 978-1-913432-52-2

Contents – Authors

Featured Artist *Imogen Hawgood*	1
Editorial	3
The Media for Poetry *Alan Gillott*	5
Editors' Corner	8
I.M. Peter Rees-Jones *Hannah Stone*	9
Illuminations *Amina Alyal*	11
This is Just to Say, for the 500TH Time *Joe Williams*	13
Destruction *John Gilham*	15
Ukraine *Susie Williamson*	17
Echoes *Rose Drew*	19
Dead Doll *Pauline Kirk*	21
Український акробат *Tanya Parker*	23
Port Mulgrave *Clint Wastling*	25
Landscape with the Fall of Icarus *Alan Gillott*	27
Taking the Long Way Home *Kathleen Strafford*	30
Calibrating the Change *Oz Hardwick*	31
Skin *Delilah Heaton*	32
Post-Procedure *Peter Datyner*	33
Apology to a New-Born Child *Stephen Capus*	34
Currer Bell *Miriam Sulhunt*	35
Eye to Eye *Stephanie Conybeare*	37
Haibun – Melissa *Clive Donovan*	38
Sciurus Vulgaris *Ciáran Dermott*	39
The Silence of the Books *David J Costello*	40
Spells *Kieran Furey*	42
Enjambment *Julian Matthews*	43
Mary's Weekend *David Harmer*	44
Underwater Symphony *Doreen Hinchliffe*	45
Playing the Music of Orkney *Pat Simmons*	46
Liminal *Fionola Scott*	47
Timepiece *Helen Heery*	48
Staring at the Sun *Chris Scriven*	49
The Raven and Me *Martin Reed*	50
Tenting Crows *Tracy Dawson*	51

Weatherspoons *Simon Tindal*	52
Try to Map Me, She Said *Emily Zobel Marshall*	53
Terra Incognita *Clifford Liles*	55
Unexpected Rain During the Drought, Bay Area *Lance Nizami*	56
The Watercourse Way *David Sapp*	57
Impassable Terrain *Jo Haslam*	58
Ennio Morrione *Timothy Houghton*	59
Axes of Alliance *Daniel Nemo*	60
The Trouble on Dandelion Road *Martha Glaser*	61
No Golden Book: a Birthday Nocturne *Wilf Deckner*	65
Requiem *Justin Lloyde*	68
Club *James B. Nicola*	69
Lifeboat *Mark Pearce*	70
Surprised by Death *Michael Henry*	72
Case History *Michael Newman*	73
Nordic Noir *Mary Michaels*	74
He's Dead *Ciaran Buckley*	75
In Memoriam *Colette Coen*	77
Everybody Knew *Estill Pollock*	82
At Least the Stars Remain *Mia Lofthouse*	83
***Enchanter's Nightshade* by Simon Currie** *Patrick Lodge*	89
***In Singing, He Composed a Song* by Jeremy Stewart** *Pauline Kirk*	90
***All the Men I Never Married* by Kim Moore** *Hannah Stone*	91
***What the Trumpet Taught me* by Kim Moore** *Hannah Stone*	91
***Hate Story* by Jeff Cottrill** *Amina Alyal*	93
***One Language* by Anastasia Taylor-Lind** *Hannah Stone*	94
***The Underlook* by Helen Seymour** *Patrick Lodge*	96
***The Thoughts* by Sarah Barnsley** *Mia Lofthouse*	97
***Offcumdens* by Bob Hamilton and Emma Storr** *Hannah Stone*	98
Index of Authors	100

FEATURED ARTIST
ARTIST STATEMENT: IMOGEN HAWGOOD

After halcyon formative years in Australia and New Zealand, I returned in late 1981 with my family to the more urban pleasures of Middlesbrough, a post industrial town in North East England. The culture shock was not without its trials. In my yearning for hot colours and crackling scents, some half remembered, some imagined, I became, like many young people in the mid-80s, an avid consumer of Americana. The exotic otherness of urban culture, underground music and life affirming pop rock anthems, imported film and addictive TV slowly inculcated a transatlantic yearning for the American Dream.

This is not to say the UK was a cultural no-man's land. The late seventies and early eighties had their own colours and stories. Counter Culture, Early Skinheads, Ska, and Two-Tone provided fertile ground for the imagination, but it was Americana and its long trek across the Atlantic that often blazed brightest. It was amplified, exaggerated, mythical.

As visual art became my litmus test of a culture's fecundity, I saw how the visual language of a place becomes fetishised and slightly distorted. That aching for the American lifestyle continues in contemporary culture, and it is no better made manifest than in the hyperreal art of UK painter Imogen Hawgood. Imogen's art explores the icons of Americana and the idea of 'the road' as a transitional and symbolic landscape. After spending time in LA, sketching, photographing, immersing, she is now lasering in on the American Dream, with its mythic allure of the West. Her recent work has included American landscapes and roadside imagery, and experimentation with light leaks and colour effects. The resulting collection is instantly cinematic. Composition and lighting engender a filmic, iconic style, reminiscent of a modern Hopper. Her experimentation with photography leads to painterly exposure flaring around the edges of her canvases, and random objects found by the roadside inspire a visual acuity akin to some of the great photorealists of our time. The propulsive night culture of LA, Sunset Strip, Las Vegas, and the dusty unwinding of the American highway, are sumptuously depicted in her 'Cinerama Dome', 'The Broadway Hollywood', 'Las Vegas Double Exposure', and 'Freeway Underpass' with an exactitude that has enamoured her to international collectors.

She says, "The freedom of the American open road has been a powerful image for generations on both sides of the Atlantic, representing for some self-discovery, for others a path to redemption. Through the use of my own photography, as well as found footage, the images I create juxtapose an air of nostalgia with contemporary viewpoints. I often use the interior of a car as a frame through which to view a passing landscape and try to capture a sense of movement through my composition and use of colour and lighting."

Imogen has exhibited at the New Light exhibition at Scarborough Art Gallery and at the Holt Festival in Norfolk. In 2020 she was shortlisted for the ING Discerning Eye, John Hurt and Sworders art prizes, and in 2021 she was 'highly commended' in the watercolour category at the Broadway Arts Festival competition. Most recently, Imogen has exhibited artwork at the Vestige Concept Gallery in Pittsburgh, Pennsylvania, According to McGee gallery in York, and Society of Women Artists Annual Exhibition, Mall Galleries London.

Greg McGee

PAGES OF ARTWORK

Mel's Drive In	29
99¢ Store	41
Las Vegas Pioneer Clib	54
Palm Springs Light Leak 1	66
Palm Springs Light Leak 2	67
Aero Theater	81
1965 Chrysler	88
Nightfall	Cover

Editorial

Much of the time since I wrote my last editorial has been spent lying down. After months of evasion, the endless ducking and diving, the masks and tests, and fingers crossed, the Covid demon caught up with me – and, like some evil succubus, has been reluctant to depart. Since this protracted health scenario causes not only physical but mental exhaustion, don't expect too much in the way of clever thoughts in this piece. I do, however, have a growing collection of snaps of cats joining me in yoga nidra. I am also considering identifying as a Victorian invalid, if that is an option, and if anyone has a spare chaise-longue.

My stalwart teams of readers and reviewers have ploughed on, despite the absence of much by way of editorial steering, and to them, as ever, my grateful thanks. I am delighted to welcome Chris Campbell to the team of reviewers (you will see his reviews begin to appear in coming months), and Mia Lofthouse as both a reader of submissions and reviewer; you will see from the quality of her work in this issue that she possesses a fine command of language, and will be on the lookout for that in the entries she reads. And that reminds me – details of our editorial team are now updated on the website, should you want to know a bit more about us. In this issue, there is rather more of me than usual in the review section, because several of our regular reviewers were not available this time. I anticipate normal service will be resumed on that front in due course.

So here we are unlocked; the trees are in leaf, the sap is rising, the airport queues are growing as exponentially as Boris Johnson's Pinocchio-nasal feature. Street parties, and festivals, and sporting fixtures vie for position in the diary. And what are you folks writing about? The usual eclectic mix of love, and death, and memory; bizarre electrical occurrences; apocalyptic scenarios, with the odd bit of nature, music, and the essence of poetry itself thrown in for good measure.

Apropos of which, I would like to remind contributors that alongside flash fiction, short stories, lineated free verse, sonnets, haiku, villanelles etc, all diverse forms of writing are welcome – and that gives me the opportunity (with a slightly different hat on) to congratulate frequent contributor (and one of the plethora of York based poets) the mighty Oz Hardwick and Anne Caldwell for their very fine book *Prose Poetry in Theory and Practice*, out now with Routledge. Ever wondered about line breaks? Considering transgressing the boundaries of the forms you grew up with? Found yourself toying with gateway changes to your right hand margins? Read this book and be inspired to write prose poetry!

Our next submission window is now open (for DC 46, which will hit the decks around the end of the year). Please send paper copies to me at 109 Wensley Drive Leeds LS7 2LU. Do have a read of Alan's piece on why we ask for paper copies.

You will note that, unusually, many of our regular editorial team get a voice this time round: we decided to invite the poets on our team of editors to include one of their own pieces, or an unpublished piece they like, and say briefly what they look for in the submissions they read. In future issues we will feature what prose editors are looking for. Since I became editor I have recruited several new readers to the editorial team, bringing much younger brains to bear on the task, and including readers from the gritty Leeds context, to supplement the dreaming spires of … York. Using blind submission, (and our usual process of 'everything is read by the editor and two other editors and two of the three have to say 'yes' for it to be published') we have on occasion included pieces written by editors and reviewers of this journal in previous issues; it's usually against my religion to publish my own work, but, hey, we can all have moments of apostasy. We hope you enjoy the Editors' Corner section.

It just remains for me to wish you a 'soiling hot bummer.'

Hannah Stone

The Media for Poetry

Dream Catcher receives regular requests for submissions to be made on-line, occasionally accompanied by qualifiers along the lines of 'in this day and age.' A number of these requests come from overseas contributors who find the cost of postage to be a significant inhibitor. It is reasonable therefore to offer our thinking behind the present method of submissions, and why change will be gradual and carefully monitored.

Dream Catcher was founded in 1996, and by 2009 had in excess of 300 subscribers and was stocked by Borders Bookshop. In that year, Borders collapsed, a victim of successive leveraged buyouts, the process that has pretty much destroyed the local newspaper industry over the last few years. Borders' failure had a desperate impact on the morale of the *Dream Catcher* team, and led in turn to a slow-down in the periodicity of the magazine.

The York poetry community has always felt that *Dream Catcher* was a York publication and gathered together to offer editor Paul Sutherland whatever help he needed to keep *Dream Catcher* alive. Paul's biggest problem was the cost of developing and printing the magazine in the context of the much-reduced income and the rapidly dwindling Arts Council grant.

In 2011 Stairwell Books was approached to provide the preparation and printing infrastructure at a fraction of the cost. At that time we established an editorial board to reduce the load on Paul by pre-screening submissions to reduce material from which he selected the material for each issue. This team filtered some 3000 submissions going back several years.

In 2014 Paul asked us to take on full responsibility for the magazine. The informal board selected a new editor, and established the submissions process. The issue of electronic submission was debated at the time and deferred: none of the team wanted to stare at a screen for hours at a time and the new editor wanted his input to be on paper. The economics did not support the cost of printing every poem in either time or money so the postal submission die was cast. Not the least, being that it is hard to doodle on a screen, draw marginalia or underline key passages, or even violently deface offending material.

In 2018, the editor retired and the next editor wanted to update our submissions infrastructure and we researched both third-party solutions and simple home-grown mechanisms. It became clear that without a significant dip into public funding a third-party solution (such as Submittable) was not viable or the magazine's sticker price would need to significantly increase, and we would also have to charge contributors significantly more than a first-class stamp to submit. A subset of the editorial board were willing to accept softcopy contributions and we opened up electronic submissions by email to overseas contributors.

What did we learn? Well, the quality of contributions dropped alarmingly. Anyone who has a Twitter or Facebook feed will understand the seductive nature of free access to internet services. Secondly, it is amazing how many overseas contributors live in the British Isles. Thirdly, online submissions are much harder to administer and the task can become overwhelming. Finally, it is astonishing how many writers have a poor understanding of how email and word processors work. For security reasons we asked for submissions in the body of the email, not as attachments, and we were surprised at the degree to which some email software adjust the message text. All emails insert non breaking spaces as triggers to the receiving client. Also, because some of the infrastructure software strips out contiguous spaces, an indent of five spaces becomes one space and four ' 's. That, and stripping out blank lines and splitting long lines into two meant that administration not only had to keep track of an increasing workload, also had to stitch poems back together. The final straw was when we published two poems as one.

We retired hurt.

In the mean time we have learned a great deal from research on perception. It seems generally accepted now that we use a different part of our brain to read from a screen than from paper and our analytical facilities are similarly affected. *Dream Catcher* is a print magazine and it makes sense for the editorial infrastructure to be paper based. In our role as general poetry publishers, a book that looks good when read online suffers greatly when printed for editing. As part of our publication process, any manuscript that looks halfway promising is always printed and reread on paper.

It makes sense. We are the product of millions of years of evolution and our aural senses developed long before we began to speak. Even though tribal oral histories were committed to paper, oral dissemination has proven the most effective. The church's most successful form of communication is the sermon and for politicians, the speech.

Electronic communication is a recent phenomenon and our brains are not yet attuned to critically analyse what is read online. Ideas that we receive on our social media feeds are accepted which, were they presented in a newspaper, would be rejected as risible. Yet it is seductive to assume words on the screen are the same as words on paper or even in the ear. They are not.

Our current editor, for reasons of health and well-being, does not have the capacity to navigate the high level of screen based activity that would be required to accept online submissions from everyone, nor the disposable income to print off every offering.

Finally, a few words on infrastructure. We briefly flirted with the idea that we could dispense with print entirely and become an online magazine. The idea soon lost traction: the average life of an online magazine appears to be between 18 months and three years with a rapid drop off thereafter.

We also learned that a number of universities use *Dream Catcher* as a teaching tool, and a print copy was de rigueur.

There are other forces that lead us away from the internet. The internet is unreliable and despite its ubiquity cannot be guaranteed to continue. Politicians good and bad have their beady eye on it: there is little chance in the long term of its being unregulated. Floods in York in 2015 knocked out a big portion of the city's ability to do business transactions, on, of all days, Boxing Day, one of the biggest commercial days of the year, highlighting the risk of relying on it for essential communication. In the UK where essential infrastructure has been privatized, ownership of physical internet assets is quite murky and an adversary only needs to know where the internet nodes are to bankrupt the UK government, which now relies exclusively on electronic reporting. The original ARPAnet on which the internet is based assumed that key nodes would be in heavily defended locations. The commercial internet is not.

We at *Dream Catcher* are still looking at fair methods of making it easier to submit from abroad without breaking our budget or overwhelming the editor. The ice may be melting but not as fast as that in the Arctic.

Alan Gillott, for Stairwell Books.

Editors' Corner

Hannah writes:

I like form. I also like formlessness. I like boundaries to be pushed, whether that is of genre of writing (is it prose, is it poetry, is it prose poetry, is it flash fiction, is it a kind of sonnet, even though it doesn't rhyme, etc etc?) choice of theme or other variable. I also like to be surprised, startled, or shocked, even – so anything that smacks of cliché or is overly familiar risks feeling, to me, like it's hackneyed. I recognise that our own frame of reference is peculiar to ourselves –and that includes not only our body of knowledge but our gaps, too (I know nothing whatsoever about sport, popular music, or computer games and would honestly struggle to recognise allusions to any of these) which is where having a team of editors is helpful. One of them might see words of genius in a piece that to me is so obscure as to be almost incomprehensible. I look for craft, in all its guises – the texture and weight of language as much as any formal or recognisable literary device. And sometimes I am merely whimsical in my choices.

In this poem, I played with the sonnet form to cobble together something about how and why we cache things underground. Since I read *The Unequalled Self*, by Claire Tomalin, I had wanted to find an excuse to write about Samuel Peyps burying his Parmesan cheese to save it from the Great Fire of London. I was also very struck by attending an exhibition connected to Holocaust Survivors at Leeds Church Institute a couple of years ago; when I came to write about the funeral of my friend, Peter, I excavated both of these from my squirrel mind, to bring together the central image of the poem.

I.M. PETER REES-JONES

What defiance accompanies every burial,
those 'two fingers' to the blanket of soil;
squirrels and magpies in autumn, saving stores
of acorns, pitting sodden suburban lawns;
and all the treasures humans cache in hasty holes
as persecution or disaster looms –
Pepys, desperate to preserve his Parmesan
from the voracious great fire of London;
the reels of film thrust into toothpaste tubes
by Jews waiting for inevitable Jack-boots;
and here, with more complex motivations,
your wicker coffin, and your mother's ashes
lowered together as the final rays
jostle the greyness of the shortest day.

Hannah Stone

Amina writes:

What I look for in poetry submissions is the unpredictable, usually in terms of the language – a way of describing something I've never come across before. Often it is something different from this, though – it may be that sentences and scenarios seem to be going one way but shift gear and change direction in ways that can be highly playful; or turns of phrase that suggest the surreal, or that really examine idiom. Sensitivity to the rhythm and music of language (whether free verse or not) is also crucial. Poems that are adventurous with form and layout on the page, when well done in a way that works with the poem's resonances and suggestions, often also achieve that sense of newness. They suggest, too, a focus on the craft of writing, which is something, for me, that is at the heart of good writing of any kind, but especially perhaps in the resonant, dense, ambiguous richness of poetry.

ILLUMINATIONS

It was just an idea. We thought
maybe an afternoon by the fire,
mood lighting and warm rum,
with a pile of the old wool we both
had lots of, never properly unwound,
never knitted, never colour-matched.

We hadn't bargained for so much of it.
When we brought out our baggage
and emptied out the tangled skeins
and spread them out to look at
they filled the room like the straw
in *Rumpeltstiltskin*. Like many tongues.

The first thread was multi-coloured,
and the first pull took us nowhere
in particular, but it ran all the way
over the heap and dragged out
all sorts of other colours, and one
full skein that spun itself into a horse.

The horse galloped us away, over meadows
of St John's wort and purple loosestrife.
The sun swept its brush over the hill
and pondered and licked at its lips.
On the other side, sailors sang shanties
and we sat and dreamed of the ships.

Amina Alyal

Joe writes:

It's hard to say what it is that makes a great submission, as the best work may not have much in common, but it is important to have a good, clear writing style and to make sure your work is edited till it is the best it can be, taking care with spelling and grammar, and (especially for poetry) avoiding cliché. It may be easier to mention some of the things that are likely to stop a piece being accepted, such as: writing that only exists to express a trite or obvious point – it's OK to write about an important issue or topic, but try to do it in an original and creative way rather than relying on tropes and platitudes; writing that is obscure to the point of impenetrability – if I have no idea at all what you are saying, I'm unlikely to think your work offers anything to our readers; writing in which it is clear the author has little understanding of the setting or characters – I amm not saying you should stick to "write what you know," but you must know enough that the situation and characters feel authentic and believable, unless you are deliberately aiming for the absurd. Happy writing and submitting!

THIS IS JUST TO SAY, FOR THE 500TH TIME
after William Carlos Williams

I have taken
the poem
that was on
the internet

and which
was probably
in a book
or something

Forgive me
it is exquisite
so stark
and so cold

Joe Williams

John writes:

I try to publish the best poetry I can get hold of that is also accessible to an intelligent reader. What, to me, makes a good poem?

1. It should say something wise, interesting, moving or funny.
2. It should be "well crafted", meaning that it does something not in a straight line with words: rhythm, usually; rhyme, sometimes; metaphor, almost always; feeling, essential; and it should show, not tell.
3. Some sort of form, whether that be free verse, a sestina or triolet, or even words which form a shape on the page.
4. And it should give the reader something at first reading, and also leave something over for the next.
5. The subject can be anything: love, death, rage, the seven deadlies, cats (if you must).

If a poem doesn't do most of those things either it's wrong for the magazine or, whatever the author says, it isn't poetry. The innovative and the conventional are equally welcome (from editorial to DC 33, for which John was editor).

DESTRUCTION
"We had to destroy the village in order to save it"
                              US military. Vietnam War.

Destroying the village in order to save it…
Destroying the Donbas in order to save it.
War's old ironies played out again
across the wheat fields, the world's granary.

Bread is ever costlier, cooking oil, scarcer,
and the lines at food banks, ever longer,
yet our grey factories shake and grind,
to mill steel into tanks, shells, missiles
that will rip Ukraine and Russians apart
in mutual destruction.

Shattered houses to rebuild, shattered citizens to tend,
Ukraine's shock waves spread across the world
in an undeclared world war, a virus,
deadly for some, consumptive for all.

This war is not far away; it's in our corner shop,
its victims in our spare rooms, its pictures
malignly resident in our minds.

John Gilham

Rose writes:

I'm a political poet. I respond to poems that say something: and this does not need to be a diatribe about the awfulness of Party X [insert name here], because all poems are political: the decision to not write about "politics" is itself political. The willingness to ignore reality is wilful. Give me a clear statement about the world from a fresh angle, and I am pulled along.

Susie Williamson's poem *Ukraine* examines the reality of fleeing a full life with only what we can carry: and then interrogates our concern. My own poem, *Echoes*, was written while working daily on a large American military base, where every entry is greeted with "Welcome home!" – even when presenting what is clearly a temporary Visitor Pass. Demitri, Mohammed, and the teens in line for coffee: what are we teaching our children?

UKRAINE

A squeaky wheel makes its presence known,
With a high-pitched, intermittent, scratchy drone,
Across hours that stretch down this long road,
The wheeled case rumbles on far from home,
The hometown, Mikolive, more distant by the hour,
Bombarded by merciless Russian power,
And with lagging energy, overspent,
Our family imagine faraway Kent.

500 miles from the Black Sea,
Mum heads this fragile family,
Son, Demitri, trails the rest,
Case in tow, he's unimpressed,
By squeaky wheel and its wobbly gait,
Only adding to the heavy weight,
Arm numb from dragging his world behind,
To the future he is strangely blind.

Fur collar pulled in tight,
To ward against the frigid night,
Yellow boots, plodding, tired,
In time with distant gunshots fired,
Wide, beady, brown eyes gaze at nightly hues,
Beneath a beanie hat, speckled blue,
The wheel squeaks, falters, then squeaks again,
Will they find peace tonight, tomorrow, when?

Hordes of rucksacks, a sea of cases,
Whole lives crammed into tiny spaces,
Among thousands desperate for safe refuge,
Night drags and still they're on the move,
Rest on frozen ground through the cold hard night,
Guards take pity on the poor boy's plight,
Drape an orange striped blanket over him, so cold,
Demitri cannot feel his toes.

A few items of clothes, a few sips of tea,
Yet many are the miles on this dire journey,
And finally they cross the border,
A celebratory hot dog in welcoming Krakow,
From Poland to Paris and finally Kent,
That squeaky wheel is now jarred and bent,

Rusted in the socket good and proper,
'No more moving,' Demitri whispers.

The case is emptied and laid to rest,
And Demitri fills his plate, impressed,
By eggs and beans and milky tea,
A normal day, but not for refugees,
After shots and bombs and dead bodies, rife,
How to tell a child that they're safe,
No words to speak, Demitri picks up his pen,
Two tanks, one big with the yellow and blue flag of Ukranians.

No time for childhood when war sparks,
But for now, he plays in a grassy park,
In one place long enough to unpack,
To kick a ball with the sun at his back…
Did I say Demitri,
I meant Mohammed,
Did I say Ukraine,
I meant Syria,
Are we still listening?
Are we there yet?
Are we opening our hearts and homes to *all* stateless?
Does Demitri include Mohammed?
Is it Afghanistan, Ethiopia or the Sudan?
Or is it just Ukraine?
Heartbroken Ukraine, we weep,
We weep.

Susie Williamson

ECHOES

This is a land of war.
Guns boom, off, behind green friendly hills,
serene trees;
now the cannon;
rapid stutter of automatic anger;
rifles sniping behind termite mounds with precision;
practicing their aim.

This is where teens train to kill,
where the blandly handsome jug-jawed youngster,
in line polite to buy coffee,
maybe a Gatorade
is learning to stomp over villages
lay all to waste
to glance down from a mile high window, release
detonation
to destroy, yet go back to camp & laugh at TV
fly home to hug his mom.

This is a land of preparation and conquest.
Helicopters with mounted machine guns & rocket launchers
named for fallen foes: Apache
Comanche
Lakota
The very roads thru the base called
Indianhead
Custer
Stonewall –
We drive along paths honouring slavers and babykillers

Then, buy gas or coffee
alongside the next generation
of the polite
the shinyfaced
the uniformed
the armed

The ready.

Rose Drew

Pauline writes:

Reading submissions always feels to me like an adventure. An envelope may contain something to give me joy, or worthy run-of-the-mill poems which won't linger in my mind. The last factor is my basic requirement. 'Do I keep remembering the poem?' 'Do lines or images stay with me?' I'm not looking for any particular style or theme, and whether it does or doesn't rhyme isn't important. I want the poem to be well crafted and communicate to the reader, even if it requires several readings. (I always read submissions at least twice.) Sadly, many a good poem is spoilt by a limp or 'preachy' ending so I look at last verses closely. If the poet has found an unusual theme or approach, so much the better – so long as it works. I suppose it's like wine tasting. You can only tell whether a wine is excellent, or merely good, by savouring it. There are no fixed rules. Bad poems, like bad wines, do tend to stand out but thankfully Dream Catcher doesn't get many of those.

DEAD DOLL

Face down, plaits flared,
the doll shocks. Cloth arms reach out
towards bracken. A check skirt flares,
red against nettle.

She interrupts our walk,
directs to an upturned playhouse,
and a child's tent flapping loose.
Toys grow into grass; a tricycle lies
abandoned.

Then we see the woman:
well dressed, young, on a tree swing,
head averted, hand and hair over face.
She does not want to be known.
Quickly we look away.

Our boots scrape silence.
In a Hansel and Gretel clearing
a silver caravan waits, off road,
off sight. No car waits beside it.
We walk on, respecting grief.

But questions torment.
What happened here?
A death? A brisk Social Service visit –
'Unsuitable Accommodation',
'Unfit Mother'?

The doll cannot answer.

Pauline Kirk

Tanya writes:

I enjoy poems that take the reader behind the main events (as in Hamlet, or A Christmas Carol) and ones where I learn something. I found out recently for example – through a poem – that young girls worked as chimney sweeps in Victorian England. That was new to me; I thought only boys did that.

УКРАЇНСЬКИЙ АКРОБАТ
(Ukranian Acrobat)

Casual Spiderman squats
at the top of his pole,
announcing a girl of five, who lives in Leeds:
All the way from England!

I may not be the best at this, he murmurs,
upside down. Catching us out,
he turns from East to West, testing wind direction,
then fish-dives to a crucifix.

This season's colours matter.
Yellow scarves and sky-blue jackets
of defiant May fertility.
The crowd sways like wheat.

Tanya Parker

Clint writes:

I enjoy reading a wide variety of poems and this is reflected in the choices I make for Dream Catcher. I always like a poem which makes me think, so an intriguing title or first line which hooks the reader is a great start. Perhaps even more importantly does the poem have a satisfactory ending? If it just whimpers then it is likely to get a rejection from me. I am enthusiastic about poems which relate the writer's experiences or emotional ties to other people or places. In my workshops I emphasise the need for emotional engagement and also to involve the senses in experiencing your words. The most important thing is have a go! If you don't try, you never succeed. Just collect the rejection slips and send your poem out again. Good Luck!

Port Mulgrave

Disconnected, inaccessible,
this hamlet of flotsam and jetsam,
formed partly from sea's gifts,
the remainder descended precipitous cliffs.

Steps fly on visiting air,
bent iron frames might dare me to descend
but January's storm ripped half away,
now only fishermen brave the climb.

Shale juxtaposed against a wild fantastic sea
where seals breed, whales become beached.
A crack! Before a tumbling melange
of cliff threatens to bury these shacks.

People imagine merfolk
copulating on the strand amongst our waste.
A nereid's birth howls swept away by the storm,
colostrum rich in microplastic from their diet of fish.

I long to visit such rugged places,
to search between myth and legend.
Port Mulgrave is a memory, inaccessible
as the tropical oceans which laid down these rocks.

Clint Wastling

Alan writes:

I am looking for something that is more than just an assemblage of words on a page. A work where the writer understands that the reader is a part of the completed poem or story and I like to see the underlying craft. For rhyming poems, I look for a corresponding attention to rhythm, not the rhythm heard by the writer but the rhythm perceived by the reader.

LANDSCAPE WITH THE FALL OF ICARUS

1

I am firm in the fertile soil
Fervid only to find tendrils of water
And to enthral the rising light
I care not for the things I remark
I see only my neighbours steady beside
Grasping, like me, for water and warmth
Buds, an itch, in the growing season
Perceiving each other between our roots

2

I am and will be forever here
My fruit, the seed of me
Plants my conscience beyond
Sharing through the landscape
And under the ground

3

I fledged by the sea, brought in the belly
Of a brightly plumed bird
Every day that sea changes fierce to calm,
Blue, or green, or often hues of grey
Salt scours my scars
But today the sea is green, wind ruffles the surface
And boats, sailing slowly, pierce my awareness
I can enjoy for a moment their serenity
My roots tell me this day was different
A new myth born just a just a few heights from here
Yet nothing changed: boats blustered in the wind
Pasture changed from green to brown
Sheep remained posed in place
Their servants tending unabated.
Only the world changed.

4

When the light grows I sense the sea
To learn whether I am buffeted by winds
Or dried in heat
Or sough in the gentle breezes

Dream Catcher 45

I see always the old castle built by servants
Beaten ruthlessly by the tides
I see the stones wither and rot away
Sculpted by the winds
And the surf scars the footings:
You, my old friend, will die before I do
My roots cannot find you
There is nowhere for my children to flourish
Between you and the surf.
I cannot my dear companion save you.

I see you my sweet confrère
Looking at me – I remark you
Remarking me, not the ploughman
Nor the horse, or ships, or sheep
Not even the distant town.

5

You resemble me, your trunk clad in sheep leaves
Boughs moving slowly around
Twigs pointing, your lank leaves
Framing your crown

I see you because you see me
Budding with blossom
Alive with new life
You, your tendrils tapping the ground,
Surrounded by images.
Take root and look at me
Only at me,
You are beautiful.

Alan Gillott

Mel's Drive In

Taking the Long Way Home

Days are museums of things designed to weigh women down
Some have affairs
      pour their hearts out
      only to find gaps in their lovers' fingers
      keep screams in a jar
      avoid ginnels
      Slit wrists to view their pulse from the inside

On the long way home a whole universe exists
where women dig in pockets for pieces of themselves
finding the women they once were
      watching dandelions in the wind
      lose their mind scattering seeds
      starting in one galaxy
      and ending up in another
halfway finishing a letter to their mother
     sprout open their siren throats
     realise tragedy & silence
     grow in the same garden

Woman   Let your life spill
           like an overturned drink
           allow your screams
           to mop up names who make your mouth run dry

          Under your skirt
          lives a Freudian slip
     it's on the tip of your tongue
say it
Let pussy & armpit opinions
grow wild
    uncurl your fist of grief
    use fingertips
    focus on your breathing
    stretch everything but the truth
    love hard   love often
    & please remember
    You are alive
               Act like it

Kathleen Strafford

CALIBRATING THE CHANGE

60 is the new 40, but while I'm younger – or older – than I assume, I toss in my biblical insomnia for 60 days and 60 nights. It's that fissured cliché of loneliness in clouds, of singing fingers baked in every pie, and of electric hands making lights – 40 watt, 60 watt, what shall we do with the baby? – work overtime for nothing but a tip at Christmas. 60% of last year's admissions were unvaccinated and 40% of fatalities were down to other causes. I am figure-hugging like a red carpet dress, the odds 60/40 on becoming a meme by morning. I'm slowly figuring things out, outing figures for what they really mean, with meaning merely an accident of swallowed substance. I fail to maintain the golden mean, but 60/40's close enough and pretty as a picture of a windswept girl with crazy hair, sailing like a kite above the crashing Channel waves. Memory's nothing but slack elastic. Neodymium is the new zirconium. 60 is the new 40, but there's a blue light flashing in my rear-view mirror and I may have some explaining to do.

Oz Hardwick

Skin

There's nothing more to play a part,
there's nothing but my naked heart,
she lays content on crimson beds,
she's pure, she's true, she's candy reds.
From beat to throb she dreamt of blue,
of dancing feet, of sands I knew,
a human frame dripped star-delight,
an astral envy burned so bright –
and though my feet aren't fit to dance,
and though my soul flirts hard with chance,
and though my brain can't rule its mind,
and though my mind's not always kind,
my dismal parts can blaze anew
when skin and skin make dreaming true –
melt into me, make atoms groan –
let's go beyond just lips and bone.

Delilah Heaton

POST-PROCEDURE

Unzipped, pointing to the screen,
The whip and spank took me by surprise,
there, in the less than wholesome shadows
Of a windowless hospital cranny

Where a spurt of men come to have
Their barrenness tested in a saucer,
Like the one in which hot wire was dipped
To draw screech from blood in *The Thing* –

Or grow the disease from scratch –
In every sense a jump in culture,
To see if the 'procedure' has killed the seed.
They are not testing for lifeblood now.

I was expecting a magazine, or nothing,
But they have ways of quickening
The pulse and the straggle chomping for a bit
In its mixture of dread and weightier breath.

The nurse at reception was pretty but hard-edged,
Latent with violent signs and iron smiles
When the tenth man of the day asked her to help out.
Do they suppose their extraordinary wit is astonishing to her?

Do they think beer-bellyness and shirt-burst
Is precisely the fetish she's been craving?
I hope that wasn't a smirk playing on her lips
When without woo I handed in my contribution,
As if she thought I was one of those wankers.

Peter Datyner

APOLOGY TO A NEW-BORN CHILD

Welcome to this world of ours,
My dear – but be forewarned
That now is not the best of times
To be conceived and born.

For though we all are very pleased
You've come to join us here,
You'd probably be better off
Remaining where you were.

For reckless greed and selfishness
And other well-known vices
Have brought us to the threshold of
An existential crisis.

The trouble is we never learned
To treat our planet well;
Money to us was dearer than
The earth on which we dwell;

The trouble is we couldn't curb
Our need for lots of stuff;
However much we had before,
It never seemed enough.

And now we've all but wrecked the place
– For which we beg your pardon:
The seas are full of plastic and
The skies are full of carbon.

One half of nature's melting while
The other turns to dust;
The trouble is that no one cared;
The trouble…was it us?

I only hope you choose to live
A better life than we did;
And so for now I wish you luck
…Because you're going to need it.

Stephen Capus

CURRER BELL

In one life she was teacher's pet,
decked herself out in lacy shawls,
trimmed bonnets with pink ribbon,
wrote frantic letters in French,
her ardour unrequited.
Monsieur ripped up the pages.
Madame pieced them back together.
You may read the contents for yourself
if your curiosity is piqued.

In another life she was poor and plain,
but found kinship with her master,
mysterious and prone to dark humours.
She wanted Rochester – her passion
hell-hot as the flames that burned down
the house with his mad wife in it.
A strange Gothic tale unfolded
stirring febrile imaginations
all round middle-England.

Nearer home, in a land of deep depression
where workers toiled in Satanic mills,
she was more radical, some said.
Others discerned less sympathy
for the suffering proletariat faced
with Hobsons's choice – starve or follow
General Ludd and smash their looms,
more fellow-feeling for the spinsters
of her own sad sister-hood.

A noted novelist chronicled her life.
She was fêted around London's salons
where she was considered a novelty.
The most celebrated artists of the age
itched to portray a woman of genius,
Millais among them. She turned him down.
Instead, chose George Richmond,
whose depiction captured the beauty
of her large hazel eyes.

Thackeray hosted a dinner in her honour,
a gloomy and silent evening,

Dream Catcher 45

during which society ladies remarked
behind their fans, that she lacked charm.
The denizens of the literary world
could not wait to pin her down,
dissect her words, anatomise her heart.
They told stories about her – some true,
many of them fanciful. She was legend.

Miriam Sulhunt

EYE TO EYE

I saw myself
in a dragonfly's eye.
I was amazing
and wildly amazed
at such proof
of my existence
in an alien
aspect.

I hovered,
slowed: saw
its shadow
shadowing us both
as my life slipped inside
its slimmer than thin body
aloft on the frailest
of wings.

It felt precise
and brightly vital
being nearly-nothing
for nearly a second
containing a whole
other-lifetime
quivering
darting

until a gust took the dragonfly
off across the pond
and I stooped
to pull a weed.

Stephanie Conybeare

HAIBUN – MELISSA

Melissa was a model bee, collecting nectar for the hive, delivering sacs of pollen wedged between knees, taking her turn on the roster with the queen; shovelling her shit, feeding grubs, conscientious as any sister. But one balmy July day, while on fanning duty in the hot passages, she was jostled by one of those gay ne'er-do-well playboys, with his handsome stripes and honey-filled paunch, on his way, no doubt, to lark about with mates in the lavender garden.

> In the busy hive
> organized to be a drone
> un-industrious

But, in short, inappropriately, she fell in love and he with her, or at least with what she could provide [for who can fathom what beguiles an insect mind? From then on she was a bad bee, filching from the royal stores for him and he sipped jelly and grew fat. Of course Autumn arrived all too soon and the whole community of virtuous femininity expelled all the drones away and out and Melissa followed even though she was sterile.

> Whisper of winter
> two cold bees compressed tightly
> on my windowsill

Clive Donovan

Sciurus Vulgaris

The whole wood fattens
on dropped leaves, like a squirrel
thickening itself for winter.

Confetti-burst birch crowns tremble,
remembering their summer glory
already fading –

up and around the dirt-path curve

a flash of ruddy tan, burgundy
flecked with rusted spokes
of grey and brown, like flaked ochre
worn by weathered rock,

too small to be a fox, the pelt too close to the ground,

more like a cat, but slimmer, scurrying
stop-start between the tawny ribbons
of branch-clusters, shivering in the glitter
of the long grass

and then gone.

Ciáran Dermott

The Silence of the Books

Picking through verbiage
like a thin bird pecking
earth for fat worms,
he hadn't noticed day
give way to Dickensian
half-light, the dull
chill of sodium street
lights, the quieting world.

His world was always
quiet. He filled it
with the silence of books.
Tolstoy and Proust
and Cervantes mumbled
dumbly in the darkness while
he pencilled his thoughts
in their margins.

Soon the books became his.
He plundered their plots.
Re-wrote their lines.
Punctuated their imperfections.
Publishers scrambled to publish
the work of the Bedsit Bard
while he warmed his
pale hands in the flames
of the books he burned
to make room for the
new ones he wrote.

David J Costello

99¢ Only Store

SPELLS

My spelling was impeccable
till learning Spanish made it friable.
It was dictionary-at-elbow time
forever from then on,
all Latinated uncertainty and suggestion
and, now that old friend Age is setting in,
withdrawals from the memory bank begin
and surefire Doubt, unwelcome lodger,
determinedly settles in.

Kieran Furey

ENJAMBMENT

In a Monday jam
And I think – enjambment
If only like a poem I could move my
car, to another line
Head to the beach
Soak my feet
In unstressed syllables
Curl me into a tiny shell
While waves of punnery wash
Over me
Carry me to an island of alliteration
Where winds of consonance blow
Breezy. With endless shores of

Line breaks

and space

(sansthismindlessimperialchase)

To rest my weary assonance
Finally forever free to craft my perfect pathetic sonnet to thee
And devote the remaining days to the rhythm of the pentameter, iambic
Rather than drown in this da-dum da-dum da-dumb
Traffic.

Julian Matthews

Mary's Weekend

One Saturday on Kent House Road,
my Grandmother fell. I was seven.
Her built-up shoe snagged the pavement,
tipped onto her back she coughed for breath.
I started to scream, she tried to laugh
Don't worry, bach, I'll soon be on my feet.
But she wasn't; a neighbour helped her up,
found her stick, checked for cuts and bruises.

The next day she was elbow deep in flour
Trex, eggs, currants, some milk,
slapping welsh cakes onto the bakestone,
its face flat and grey, like the slate they'd hung
round her neck for not talking English at school.
That said NW, not the chalked ten and six
my dad had spotted outside an iron mongers
up Sydenham high street, a real bargain.

As she baked, Grandma spoke in Welsh
slowly and loudly so I'd catch her drift.
I couldn't of course, even when she pointed
to plates and cupboards, the spoon I was licking,
like the day before, I was lost at sea.
She smiled, rubbed dusty hands over her apron,
let the scent of newly minted cakes, stacked
like coins, do the talking.

David Harmer

Underwater Symphony

No tongue is strange to the rhythm of waves
that lull the skeletons of wrecks and all
the drowned, transforming empty skulls to caves
for curious fish. The constant rise and fall
and ripple of tides is its own music, a swell
of sound echoing from the deep's remains.
The rattle of bones, the tolling of a bell
from a sunken ship, the clank of prisoners' chains
or clink of ancient coins – these resonate
with every haunting cry of those who crossed
the sea and perished, uniting to create
a harmony, a symphony of the lost.
Down here, a thousand languages are blended
into one, every dissonance ended.

Doreen Hinchliffe

PLAYING THE MUSIC OF ORKNEY
Homage to Peter Maxwell Davies

Orkney Wedding. With Sunrise
Maxwell's Reel, With the Northern Lights

He knew that whisky and wonder
could lean together, arms
lovingly round each other,
that wedding guests could reel out
into a dawn that danced
and leaped to the bagpipe skirl,
that the Northern Lights could pulse
with the stomps of a village hall hop.

Trumpet Concerto

Knew that where our feet,
striding or dancing, touch
the earth we're held, even loved.
But respected the panic of rocks,
their straining, their tumbling. Dug music
out from stone with a shovel
to hurl it up roaring against
the roar of bare-boned cliffs.

Piccolo Concerto

Unanchored as air, his notes
muse on loneliness, trust
their way over low green land,
unafraid of sadness,
dance to the drums, skip
from one wave-tip to the next.
In the end he slid them deep
into silence, let them let go.

Farewell to Stromness

Felt the sea lapping and gnawing
smashing and nibbling,
waiting restless and patient.
Let it bear him out and away.

Pat Simmons

LIMINAL

If I'm granted I'll ride
that soft ebb-flow follow
tidelines watch spindrift
trail the selkie's silver wake

scuttling crabs sleeping sandbars
will graze my knees in quiet farewell
my belly bladderwrack-bound

else I will rage rage azure rip-tides
defy headwater seek rapids
I will harness undertow pound my way
tsunami trees overwhelm crannogs

never treading head high
I will savour salt and fear
  collapse time

Fionola Scott

TIMEPIECE

Tilt back its face to catch the light;
one long scratch across the glass
particles of dust trapped beneath.
I have loved this watch, patched it up
stapled in place the unstitched strap
that possesses the particular curve
of my wrist, and in the row of little holes,
one in the middle grown biggest.
Only metal and leather have tarnished,
flat-lining batteries have been replaced,
hands wound to the current time.
But nothing in memory has sullied or worn
the moment I learnt to tell the time,
when Dad and I jumped in the car, drove
to Nairobi town and on foot, threaded
our way through Saturday streets,
found the shop on River Road to buy
my very first watch; all up to the minute
with its shiny pink strap, tiny white face,
the second hand ticking loud as my heart.

Helen Heery

Staring at the Sun

I've woken to the warmest slanting ray
and felt the gentle touch of morning light.
With all the inspiration of the day,
the stars are dimmed that I once thought so bright.
The empress of the day, goddess of dawn,
for your inspection all the earth's arranged
and to your golden radiance I'm drawn,
a satellite whose orbit can't be changed.
From such a distance yet to such effect,
you rule my world, hypnotic orb of fire,
I claim the right to worship, not expect
rewards beyond perfection to admire.
No sight could be more beautiful or fair
yet so much brighter than my eyes can bear.

Chris Scriven

The Raven and Me

Only the raven and me this morning
on top of North Hill
as he shows me how he can ride the wind,
flapping about me,
wondering why on earth I'm here.

I shiver in russet anorak
and not enough layers to keep out the cold.
I can't make out his black ruby eye
alive in that arrow of jet black head
but he can see mine

as he goes about me, takes me in,
reads my worries – health and money –
finds me altogether a puzzle.
To me he's shadow, silhouette,
death bird, wise bird, corvid king

of his turf-rock castle.
He escorts me from his territory
as I descend to my warm house-prison,
triumph his farewell croak, his guttural oath.
Or could it be laughter?

Martin Reed

Tenting Crows

Village children skipped school again that day:
It was autumn – their hats were stuffed with straw.

Census records some employed Tenting Crows.
I imagined A-framed wooden clothes-horse,

draped flaps of Grandad's gabardine trench coat
and grandma's taxidermy fox fur stole.

I thought about Trespass and a Gore-Tex
family tent spreadcorvid on tenterhooks.

After harvest, sheaves of corn stacked in stooks
had been gathered in. Threshing was over.

'The Fall of Icarus' meant nothing
to those children wildly flapping their arms,

aspiring to rise up as air dancers.
Flailing limbs lifting them over furrows

in that harrowed field. A murder of children
nailed a gory crucifixion of crows.

Cruelly impaled on a stake, they cawed
warnings until the threshing was over.

Tracy Dawson

Weatherspoons

Flowsnakes are causing bailtacks
from Madcaster to Tiddlesbrough.
Wail hornings mean Dane relays
from Diverpool to Lover
and there are flightning lashes
between Owbridge and Tripswich.
In nappier hews, bunseams have
cleared shitter bowers blocking
the Fartford-Deltham piebass
itch windicates a piled massage
before a soiling hot bummer.

Simon Tindal

Try to Map Me, She Said

Try trace my contours with your pen
draw my ridges, hidden coves
commit to paper the features of
my hills and valleys

But you will only find my outline
your charts will not determine
the storms that carve my bays
the stillness of my caves

I shall write you then, he said
in sonnets and in prose
distil in verse wrinkles between brows
and harmony of leg and arm and waist

Try to write me and you'll miss
the beating of my temple
the smell I leave behind
on my side of the bed
the shape the battered backs
my old slippers take
the sharpness of
my early morning breath

Only burnt beneath your fingers
will you feel the anger
swelling in my belly
in days before I bleed
the answer to what makes me
woman

My salty fissures
and my cracks
in words cannot be tracked
live unchartered, uncontained
beyond a world of facts
so this body will remain
unmapped

Emily Zobel Marshall

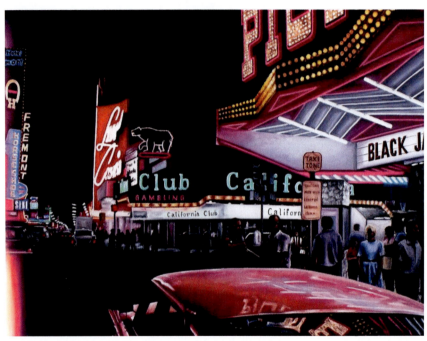

Las Vegas Pioneer Club

Terra Incognita

This is God's own country, he says to his son
through fierce tears. But the terracotta dirt
is dry as clinker. A leafless ghost gum
fingernails the sky as insectile heat
enfolds him, intimate as death, feasting
on sweat. Out of sight, in his scungy kitchen,
his tap drips. Once. From out of the hot nowhere
a zephyr swirls. A flyscreen door bangs.

His rows of wheat lie flat like torn up shrouds.
Each full dark the empty dingoes stray in,
tongues lolling. Their tattoo of want a necklace
round his house. He whispers to his son: *Never
seen the like of this.* But his son is out,
a truckie hauling water to the towns.

Clifford Liles

Unexpected Rain During the Drought, Bay Area

The streets are shining soaking wet
The raindrops ping where drainpipes flatten out

Nearby: empty reservoirs, flat bottoms green-grass-covered
Deer are there now, gathering to drink from streams meandering

The rain itself is drunk by thirsty earth
There's little chance that lakes will soon return

No rain can be enough to saturate this porous land
No rain can be enough to turn our valleys back to sloshing tubs

Old Noah's Flood alone could change ravines here back to waterways
And desert-style flash-flooding never happens here-abouts

The fertile soils are left from forest floors so thick with seeds
The soil's a spongy loam that gobbles moisture

The loam expands with water, it will tighten to the roots
It draws the moisture, precious moisture; puddles never form

This is Northern California's earth, where redwoods covered all the land
The stands of redwoods stretched from Bay to ocean

They left a twiggy duff that sits beneath the rows of homes
That duff was once the aquifer, the earth's true California water-hold

And now we have the giant empty grainy reservoirs
Deer are gathering on the greening bottoms

House-wards, raindrops ping where drainpipes flatten
The streets are shining soaking wet.

Lance Nizami

THE WATERCOURSE WAY

I didn't listen when,
a very long time ago,
Lao Tzu and Siddhartha
matter-of-factly, kindly
informed me that the chaos
of my mind is likely
the origin of my suffering,
my worry, my obsession
or rather my attempt
to harness it is my madness.

Eventually, painfully,
I discovered my mind
is not fabricated of levers
and gears, wires and switches.
It is a faulty analogy,
a dreadful misconception,
to view my head as an oily
machine or a set of circuits,

to assume there's an orderly
schematic to apprehend,
to follow. My mind, my mind
is as nature, moves as water
(the sage's *Watercourse Way*)
and acts accordingly, defying,
pushing at artificial edges.

Occasionally my mind
is routed by a pipe or sluice.
However, dams and levees fail.
To grab ahold of it is a futile,
illusive endeavor. So silly.
As anyone, from time to time
I am damp with a few tears
or drenched in a sudden storm.

David Sapp

Impassable Terrain

You text me in the middle of the night
from somewhere in the mountains.
You've forgotten we're six hours behind
and I don't say. You tell us your next destination
but we've checked the route already;
rockfalls, passes blocked, weather closing in.
You'll make the journey anyway
impelled by a need I can't identify.
'Son,' I want to ask, 'What are you searching for?'
But perhaps you don't know, although some god
somewhere may have the answer.
But we don't believe in gods, do we? Demons
are another matter; the ones that left you raging,
then for months hopeless and afraid;
our footloose boy with no good ground
beneath him. Even then, snow pale
and strained, your impulse was to go.
And now there in your sights,
improbable blue peaks, a sky so cold
and bright it hurts to look. So I don't tell you
how our own is creeping grey, how mild our July,
its few days of heat, and how tonight it rained.
I can hear it through the open window
falling on the garden, and now I've lost
the thread of sleep. I don't tell you this either,
or how I've planted sweet peas, tended them
like children, and they've flowered, pink,
deep plum and white, reaching skywards
though the trellis. They smell like honey.
And I'm glad of the rain, its quiet fall,
still cool when I go out. I say none
of this, trust you to keep your own
good sense, your father's instinct
for direction. And I wish you heat, rain,
when you need it; the smell of honey. I wish
you godspeed. I wish you your blue mountain.

Jo Haslam

ENNIO MORRIONE
his scores for Leone westerns

Bullet-blood
doesn't burst out
in the '60s films. It's in our minds, a diabolical child
of blue sky and blinding gold sun. It is glare
expanding
–in soul–
what it touches
and finds speech in the men below.
A rose door
opens from a cirrus cloud
mid-day (when sun boils like an angry man
barely under control)
and lets loose
whispers of mayhem. Van Cleef, Volonté,
and *The Man With No Name*
who holds the Colonel's pocket watch.
The slow pace
takes fight into
reflection, where peace might be expected
in halfway times.
But here it's an anvil cloud
seen from a distance, promise
of chaos, brain
ungrasping
dimension. The blur
is truth. How, in our age, can one speak of revenge.
In deep-sea thermal jets
miles below light,
under pressure
indescribable,
life fights.
Two men ready themselves, circling each other
till sun won't block their eyes.

Timothy Houghton

AXES OF ALLIANCE

What spark there is seems to light the scene from either end.

In an interpreted world, you see what *appears*,
each day more, or less.

The tree shadows on mountaintops are large caterpillars.

The compound eye a vending machine.

The train window a skyway in which an arrow shoots through space.

When the arrow line is active
it creates divisions into imaginary planes–

yet when moving round a vacuum
you're hermetically sealed in

not all that much changes …
Nothing happens off the screen.

The layers and the dots are yours.

There's no other law but the one you yourself have devised.

The initial impulse is extracted from
the new identity assumed   [feelings you're no longer feeling,

stimuli converted and proportioned
to avoid disturbance]

twelve-bar pneumatic reflex
in the condensation chamber

circulating like an echo

mornings when the mind is clumsy
and bumps into things.

Down the mountain
a man and a woman, light and darkness, slowly approach in a canoe.

Daniel Nemo

Note: *When the arrow line is active it creates divisions into imaginary planes* –
in reference to *The Thinking Eye*, by Paul Klee

THE TROUBLE ON DANDELION ROAD

It was a Saturday morning when Mr. Molotov was electrocuted. His hand was stuck to the ToastMaker 101, to the exposed wire by the crumb tray, and the rest of him was stuck fast in a stance of mild surprise. All he could do was think, so he thought on his sins and his failures. *Sometimes I drink out of the toilet bowl like a dog. I can't touch my toes. All of my bonsai trees are dead. One time I saw Bigfoot at Poundstretcher but nobody believed me. I wish I'd bought the WaffleMaker 120. I don't even like toast.* He could smell his own burning skin and burning hair which smelt like bacon butties and made him even hungrier. *Sizzle sizzle, Mr. Molotov,* he thought, disgusted, as the electricity coursed through him. He thought of all his animal properties: his chicken skin and his reptile smile, his beady eyes and his presently pig-like state. Pig Molotov, he'd call himself if he survived, which he was seriously beginning to doubt. Mr. Molotov lived at Number 12 Dandelion Road. Ironically, twelve was his lucky number. The ToastMaker 101 had twelve toast settings from 'cold' to 'charred'; right now he and his toast were at number six, 'lightly crisped'. Six was half of twelve which was half of twenty-four which was his present age, and there were twenty-four hours in a day, but it was eleven o'clock now, so there were really only thirteen hours left of it, and thirteen was an unlucky number, and no wonder, since here he was getting his brains fried for breakfast.

Bob Whiskerson, who lived at Number 14 Dandelion Road, was the first to hear Mr. Molotov yelling on this otherwise unremarkable Saturday morning. Bob Whiskerson, despite being an integral member of the Neighbourhood Watch, did not know Mr. Molotov very well. In fact, he only knew Mr. Molotov's name because of misdelivered post that had come through his letterbox once. Bob had, out of love and nosiness, opened the letter only to find that Mr. Molotov was being invited to the Bingo League's Second Annual Christmas Party. It was that same nosiness that brought him to Number 12 on Saturday morning, and when he saw Mr. Molotov stuck to the toaster and smouldering, it was that same love that made him forget all of his common sense. He reached for Mr. Molotov, and tried pulling him away. In doing so, Bob himself felt the spark of the ToastMaker 101. The eager current pulled him close, his hand stuck to Mr. Molotov's shoulder, his face contorted into a grimace. He had been tasered once before, and this was not unlike that, but as Bob Whiskerson stood there being electrocuted, all he thought of was his successes. *I can hold my breath for two hours. I've never had chickenpox. Last winter I ran a three minute mile. This isn't how I thought I'd die. I thought I'd die choking on a wishbone at a seaside restaurant in Toulouse.*

Sally Chestnut, across the road at Number 13, glanced up at the first hint of commotion. It crashed through her window, the sound of this commotion, ending up on her kitchen floor and limping up to the table where she sat drinking a cup of tea. Though not a member of the Neighbourhood Watch, she valued the tranquility of the ordinarily trouble-free street, which right now was being grossly violated. She also smelled a faint smell of frying. Elevenses, she thought, sipping her cup of tea. She placed it back on the saucer, wrinkled her nose, and then hotfooted it across the road to Mr. Molotov's, where the first thing she saw was the front door left ajar. The next thing she saw was her two neighbours, standing in the kitchen, sizzling. Sally reached for Bob's arm, just as unthinkingly as Bob had reached for Mr. Molotov, and found herself as stuck as the rest of them. As she began to fry, Sally thought of all the things she hadn't done and couldn't do. *If this is the end, I'll never get to swim the Channel. I'll never go to Crufts or Coachella or anywhere else. This can't be it!*

Pete the Merman, who lived at Number 16, was shelling peas at the time of the incident. He usually kept to himself, and the only remarkable thing about him was his pegleg. He claimed that he had lost his leg somewhere in the Pacific Ocean, to a shark with a vendetta against him. In reality he had lost it in a lawnmower accident in the 80s, but he never told anybody that. On Saturday morning he was sitting in the garden beside his vegetable patch and thinking about lunch, when he heard a crackling sound. He could not immediately identify the source of the sound, but when he heard his neighbours yelling, he sat up straight. He screwed his pegleg back on and darted to Number 12. Arriving at Mr. Molotov's kitchen, he looked at his neighbours sparking and strung together, and grabbed Sally Chestnut's hand. His electrocution was no less vicious than the rest, and as he stood there frying, his unanswered questions spilled through his mind. *Does going to prison ruin your credit score? What is the difference between satsumas and clementines? Why do garden gnomes exist? Did I turn the dishwasher on?*

It was Number 15 who came running to the house next, woken from a weekend lie-in by the clamour at Number 12 Dandelion Road. *Wednesday's child,* Number 15 thought as he joined the chain and felt the current, *full of woe.* He was too busy thinking about his woefulness to notice his neighbours from Number 17 grabbing hold of him, and his neighbours from Number 18, and his neighbours from Number 19. Soon enough, there was a chain of people stretching from Mr. Molotov's kitchen, down Dandelion Road, across the junction, and into the main road. More and more people would attempt to break the chain, but in reaching out to help, they would find themselves electrocuted, too. At some point the fire brigade arrived, but they simply joined the chain along with the rest of Dandelion Road. Local news would later report the incident as '*the dumbest thing that's ever happened in this town*' and when it was all over, a small memorial was built to mark the human chain, which every year drew to it a few curious locals and bored daytrippers.

Harry Higgins, CEO, was on his way to a Highly Important Meeting at the time of the ToastMaker 101 incident. "I don't care," he barked into the phone, his voice straining above the car horns, "Tell them I can't come because my retinas are detaching. Tell them I have scurvy. Whatever you want. I already have one Highly Important Meeting this week. I don't have time for another." He looked out of the car window, at the commotion outside. "Who are these people? Why are they in the road?" He said it to nobody in particular, but it was the driver who leaned back and explained, quickly, about the trouble on Dandelion Road. Higgins heard a helicopter overhead which, unbeknownst to him, carried the journalists snapping pictures for tomorrow's story. He looked back at the string of people spread across the road. Like a paper doll chain, he thought. Higgins frowned, his racing mind coming to an uncomfortable standstill. He disliked the chain. He disliked it immensely. But he did not know why.

As the lights turned green and the cars remained still, Harry Higgins sat up. He pulled his face away from the car window, and took the phone out of his pocket. "I don't have time for this," Higgins muttered, fumbling with the phone. He'd had the mayor on speed dial for three years. In one minute the call was placed; in two minutes it was done. The town's power supply was switched off, the ToastMaker 101 stopped sparking, and the chain of forty-five once-electrified neighbours fell awkwardly apart. They looked at each other, sprawled along Dandelion Road, along the crossroads, along the main road, and along the front of Harry Higgins' car. The road was silent except for the sound of the helicopter, which hovered for some time high above them.

Later, Higgins sat in a conference room across town. It was too warm. Higgins wished somebody would open a window, but nobody else seemed to care. He sat rubbing his brow, his mind wandering. He lived on the top floor of a high-rise. If I were to be electrocuted, he thought, who would come to help? Would there be a neighbourly chain? He decided there would not. His next door neighbour was out of town on a balloon ride. His neighbour across the corridor had allergies and never left the house. The flat downstairs was an AirBnB and empty most of the time. He'd burn to a crisp, he reasoned. "Mr. Higgins?" somebody said, looking at him. "Do you have anything to add?" He shook his head. It had started to rain outside. The rain pelted against the conference room windows, threatening to break them; he looked at the sky, which was grey and groaning. Lightning, he realised. A single bolt, coming just for him. The minute he stepped outside of the building he would be struck by it, almost without doubt. It was the result of his meddling. His tampering. His dalliance with the town's power supply, all so that he could be at this meeting. This meeting with stale biscuits and staler conversation. He stared out of the window as the storm worsened. By now he was certain of his fate. He held his breath and balled up his fists, waiting, wondering. But nothing happened. No thunder or lightning or anything of the like. The rain, he noticed now, was stopping. The sky outside had cleared. For the first time in his long and illustrious career, Harry Higgins was glad that he had been wrong about something. He smiled and leaned back in his chair, while the rest of the conference room smiled, confused, along with him.

"So what happened to the ToastMaker 101?" Bob Whiskerson asked Mr. Molotov one evening, leaning over the garden fence. It had been some weeks since their collective electrocution, and their recollections were distant and hazy. Aside from the burning smell that hung around Dandelion Road for a while, there was nothing much that remained from the event.

"Gone," Mr. Molotov said simply, placing his garden shears on the ground with uncharacteristic vigour. He explained how he had, immediately after the incident, relegated the ToastMaker 101 to the bin. It was carried away the following Friday, which was bin day, to a recycling plant where it was crushed to pieces and turned into plastic toilet seat hinges. Bob Whiskerson nodded, seemingly satisfied, and returned to his house.

He did not know that Mr. Molotov had lied. He did not know that the ToastMaker 101 was in Mr. Molotov's pantry. It sat on the bottom shelf, hidden behind an expired pack of cornflakes. Bin day had come and gone, and Mr. Molotov's bins were decidedly toaster-free. Mr. Molotov would steal glances at the ToastMaker 101 occasionally, if he happened to need something from the pantry, or if he was cleaning the shelves, or if he was reorganising his kitchen utensils. Shortly afterwards he moved house, to a place with two flatmates and a fish tank in the living room. He left most things behind at Number 12 Dandelion Road, but he took the ToastMaker 101 with him. It was singed and blackened. It was a hazard to life and limb. It took up precious shelf space. He refused to throw it away. It was a reminder, he said when he was asked, which was rarely, because he kept it so very well concealed. It was a reminder of the human chain, he tried to explain. He would never throw it away, he said. It was the connection to Bob Whiskerson, and Sally Chestnut, and Pete the Merman, and the others living in that road, at that particular time, on that particular day. "You mean your friends?" his flatmates said, as they chatted one evening. Mr. Molotov shook his head, struggling to explain. "They weren't really my friends," he said, "but they were, well, they were *there,* you know?"

Martha Glaser

NO GOLDEN BOOK: A BIRTHDAY NOCTURNE
"Come Midnight and close this Year so rich in Tears"
(Andreas Gryphius, Sonnet XV, The Second Book)

'Saint Peter in his Heaven
Records each misdemeanour
With golden pen in a vast golden book.'
Aged three or four, this tale impressed
Itself on my unlettered mind.

And for some time thereafter,
With pencil stub and cast-off diary,
I too recorded all who had
Incurred my holy wrath:
'I put you in my golden book!'

These days, more than one half
A century later, mostly my own
Shortcomings fill the pages,
Mingling dreamscapes in turmoil with
Subconscious fears churned up.

An over-wakeful mind in the small hours,
Charting recurring pain and glimpses
Of physical debility concealed,
Of chronic loathing, anger, and disdain,
Tersely recorded, in one unholy mess.

Wilf Deckner

Palm Springs Light Leak 1

Palm Springs Light Leak 2

REQUIEM

In 1785
Friedrich Schiller wrote a poem
called 'Ode to Joy'

in 1824
Beethoven used the structure of the poem
for the final movement
of his ninth symphony
Ode to Joy

in 2018
When my Joy died
I used the structure of the music
to make a poem to her memory

Ode to Joy

Bleak December brought us sadness
Bitter winds and lonely nights
End of this year, a fearful season
Harsh and dark as winter bites
We shall mourn you
And celebrate you
After winter comes the thaw
We shall plant seven cherry trees for you
This will be our Ode to Joy

Justin Lloyde

CLUB

If you get here I'll be
glad you got here
but if you don't see me
don't think I'm not here.
Since I'm not allowed to look outside
I hope you'll try to look inside.
If the line is long, chat
up The Bouncer, that
should do it. See
if maybe he
will let you sneak
a little peak.
If I manage to
see you at The Gate
I'll wave then wait
for you.
I don't know when
or even if you'll appear
but it won't be Heaven
here
until then.

James B. Nicola

Lifeboat

A large lifeboat floated in the middle of a calm sea. In the background could be seen a luxury liner in flames, sinking beneath the surface of the water. Two men sat in the lifeboat, each eating a can of beans. Edmund Graves had an oar across his lap. Victor Stavenger had one at his feet. Neither man spoke.

Suddenly a hand gripped the rail. A man pulled himself up from the water; he was sopping wet and breathing heavily.

Stavenger quickly grabbed the oar at his feet and leapt to the side of the boat. He began to beat the man back into the water. It took many whacks, as the man was struggling for his life. Stavenger beat him about the head, the shoulders, the chest, the hands. Edmund calmly continued to eat his beans while watching this outburst. The man over the side never made any noise; he just struggled silently until he finally disappeared into the inky depths. Stavenger sat down and resumed his meal.

Edmund finished the bite he was chewing, then spoke: "I'm glad I got to the boat before you did."

They ate for a moment in silence. The man's head appeared once again. Stavenger took up the oar again and clubbed him about the head and shoulders, forcing him back into the water. Once again, it was a long, drawn out process. When it was over, Stavenger sat.

Edmund looked across at his fellow passenger. "You know you're using up more calories keeping him out of the boat than you're saving by depriving him of rations."

"It's the principle."

There was a brief pause as they continued to eat.

"Is this your first voyage?" asked Edmund.

"No," said Stavenger. "I sail all the time."

"Pleasure?"

"Business."

"Really? What do you do?"

The man reappeared. His left arm clung desperately to the side of the boat while his right hand waved a fistful of money.

Stavenger took up the cudgel once again and beat him back into the water. As before, the man never said a word, just struggled in desperate silence until he finally disappeared. Stavenger resumed his seat.

"Sorry," he said.

"That's quite alright," said Edmund. "You were about to tell me what you do for a living."

"Oh. I write travelogues. You know, 'The Joys of an Ocean Voyage.' That sort of thing."

"How interesting."

"What about you? Done much traveling yourself?"

"I've been on a few cruises," said Edmund. He peered into the water where the man had disappeared. "None like this, though."

"I know," said Stavenger. "This *has* been pretty rough. This reminds me of that story – you know – six men in a boat, who do you eat first?"

Edmund lifted his oar menacingly. "Don't expect any votes until you let some more people in the boat."

Stavenger set aside the can of beans he had been eating and looked up at the sky. "It'll be night soon."

Edmund followed his gaze. "I guess so."

"At least the weather is calm. I wonder if they'll be able to find us. The rescue ship I mean."

"I don't know," said Edmund. "Do you think the captain had time to get off a distress call?"

"I hope so. We ought to be okay as long as we stay in the shipping lanes. Someone will come along eventually."

A hand stretched up from the water, fingers outspread like a leafless tree; trembling, it grabbed the rail.

Stavenger ran to the edge of the boat and violently stomped the fingers. It took a while, but the hand eventually disappeared. Stavenger stood with his foot poised a moment, then resumed his seat.

"I didn't want to disturb you," said Edmund, "but isn't that a rescue ship over there?"

Stavenger squinted at the horizon. "Maybe. It'll do anyway."

He lifted his can of beans, finished the last few bites, and tossed it aside. Edmund picked up one of the bags.

"Anything you want to take with us?" he said.

"Nyah," said Stavenger. He peered at the horizon. "How soon do you think they'll be here?"

"About fifteen minutes. Maybe less."

Stavenger nodded as if the answer satisfied him. He leaned back against one of the bags and clasped his hands behind his head.

"You know," he said, "it wasn't such a bad cruise after all. I definitely think I'll recommend it to my readers."

He propped his feet up, closed his eyes, and smiled peacefully as he awaited the arrival of the rescue ship.

Mark Pearce

SURPRISED BY DEATH

A grey peace has descended over the basilica.
A black estate car waits at the west entrance.

We go in by the disabled door to Gounod's *Ave Maria*.
Six men exit the Lady Chapel, performing
their shoulder-balancing act with a light-oak coffin.
The French let birth and death go hand-in-hand.

We ponder our minuteness
in the antiquity of things. You search
Saint-Seurin, Bordeaux on your iPhone.
Outside, the casket slides into the hearse like a drawer.

The inmates of grief prepare to leave
and a man invites us to the *cimetière*.
We would go if this were Paris.
Instead, we sit out for morning coffee.

You order *café allongé*.
I order *café crème*,
am disappointed at the small amount
and drink it in one fell swallow.

There's a time for coffee and a time to refrain from coffee.
There's a time for death and a time to think of dying.
I'm reminded of the busts on tombs at Père Lachaise
looking surprised at the *blunder* of their *being dead*.

Michael Henry

CASE HISTORY

The old woman in Ward 7
Knew she was a prophet in Israel.
No amount of cajoling
Would convince her otherwise.
She watched seagulls
Heading for the Red Sea,
Saw in *sedum spectabile*
The Burning Bush.
She knew Jerusalem
Lay beyond the perimeter wall –
Only, they never let her out.

One day a fresh psychiatrist
Started to ask questions
About her childhood.
Where was she born.
Where did she go to school.
'But I was taught by Moses,'
She declared.
Then, sensing a German accent,
'Why did you do it?'
'Do what?' asked Dr Steiner.
'Gas the inmates.'

Michael Newman

In this story, everyone is watched. In real time and continuous recording. Both by the crime-boss on his computer and by the police. On big screens round the investigation hub, in grainy half-tones, a woman can be seen inside her apartment, pleading or bargaining with her hostage-taker. Out on the street, plain-clothes officers confer with uneasy-looking local informers. Huddled down an alley a SWAT team waits.

With what complacency we also watch.

Suppose my house had been fitted up with cameras. Imagine each room viewed from the corners, and me registered, in all my repetitive, routine movements, my to'ing and fro'ing. Picture the kitchen which is also the living room; the reaching and bending, the opening and closing. While the digital tablet on the top of the fridge glows out its message in pale letters, *Now it's Tuesday, Now it's Wednesday*....

You'd have to spool through for hours and hours, to find anything significant.

~

I've done my share of killings, of course. Mostly through an agent, paid for the job. Of the rat, for instance, which had made itself a nest under the bath – chewed-up newspaper littered with shells (from cobnuts among the still-life props in the studio). It had been waking me early every day with its scrabbling and sorting. Poor little thing! But that's not what I thought, finding, one morning, a skirting board blackened with oil from its pelt.

The bones will be under the loose floorboards. With mummified flies, that hatched from the corpse as it was decomposing.

~

I dreamed last night that my brother came home. After all these years. It was the occasion of a big funeral – his, oddly, although it was decades he'd been gone. Dozens, if not hundreds, of people on the street for this event and then – there he was, smooth-faced, silent, in a gray double-breasted suit. I didn't ask him where he'd been all these years – what did it matter? I've asked before – he never says anything.

Mary Michaels

HE'S DEAD

He is dead

His shrivelled dead body
Is being laid in the dead earth
(*the earth died when it heard he was dead*)

His friends have shattered their legs with hammers
As a mark of respect, and crawl face first
Across the land to weep at his grave,
They wound their faces on every stone they can.
His million slaves hang themselves on their chains
Knowing no other master could ever be like him.
The pigeons all drown themselves in rank canals,
The nightingales dive into speeding cars on motorways,
Lion and lamb lay down in the garage
And stick a pipe in the exhaust

The people, as one, the people pluck out
One eye each at least, and several teeth,
For miles they queue
For traces of his last jizz
To pour over breakfast cereal
Drips of his last piss
To ferment into alcoholic beverages
The scrapings of his last excrement
Frozen and scooped into ice cream cones
The young and the young at heart come running
When they hear the tune

At his gravestone his wives gnaw and tear
At each other's jugulars, each wishing
To be the one name carved under his

His mistresses are kept
At gunpoint behind the gate
With all their little bastards in tow
Faces mashed and meshed to look like Daddy,
One of the newest slips through a preprepared tear
Shoulders through the crowd
Rips a ***AT THIS POINT CERTAIN***
SECTIONS OF IMAGERY
GO FURTHER THAN

CAN BE Putative Father ***EXPECTED***
TO BE upon the mourners
REASONABLY TOLERATED AND SO
WILL REMAIN FOR THE TIME BEING
REDACTED as much as they can
The last of him they may ever taste

The rain is pouring down on the grave
The rain is pouring down on the dead earth
God just can't help it
He just can't stop crying
God says
"*IT IS BETTER NOT TO KNOW*
WHAT GOD SAID"

The sun has had enough
It shoves a shotgun up its throat
Points the handle toward the moon
And tells it to pull the trigger
The moon pulls the trigger
The sun's brains are blown out all over everything
And nothing ever happens again

Ciaran Buckley

In Memoriam

His name, printed black on cream, stops my heart for a moment.
A lovely man, sorely missed. Always, Celia.

It is not my style to make public my grief. Of course, there was a death notice, people had to know, especially once the phone calls became too perfunctory, and there were too many whose details were out of date.

The children set up a Facebook page or memorialised their father's or some such. I don't know. And I drew the line at Snapchat, though they maybe still did it, behind my back. They said it was no different from how I chose to let my friends know, but I felt it was not formal enough for death.

Celia, whoever she is, must have known that my friends read that paper, and Andrew's colleagues. We are at an age when we check the obituaries just to make sure we're not listed. And funerals are about as close as many of us get to a social life these days.

It was Gina who first mentioned it, as I knew she would, always looking to get one over on me.

'Did you see yesterday's paper?' she asked, almost before she sat down in the lounge.

'Yes,' I said, 'how nice that he has been remembered so fondly.' That flummoxed her, took her a moment to form her next question.

'So, you know this Celia?'

'Of course,' I said, though I don't, 'now shall we have some wine – I'm sure you can make an exception, given the circumstances. I think we should toast Andrew's memory, it being a year and all.'

She didn't know what to do after that, or she forgot all about it, and I rather enjoyed our lunch, keeping the conversation spinning towards, and then away from, that blasted message.

The children were next to enquire; David being nominated as spokesman. I was surprised they were even aware of it; I had certainly not drawn it to their attention. He prevaricated, the only skill he seemed to have, and I would have snapped and told him to hurry up if I hadn't seen something of Andrew in him. At least his stumbling gave me time to think. Of course, there had been nothing else on my mind for days, but what to tell the children, that was something quite different.

I had started my investigation the only way I knew, by pulling open the cupboard in the room to which I am more or less confined and taking out the photo albums and shoe boxes filled with mementos – christenings, big birthdays, anniversaries, and there, in the only one that lacked a label, the sympathy cards.

I hadn't read them properly at the time, I think it was deemed too upsetting; and I had delegated the task of sending out the memorial cards to Marissa and Dawn. They tried to share little snippets with me, but at the time, I was too busy trying to figure out a way forward, to have any time to look back. Now, I took it slowly, even reading the crass verses, secular and religious, before taking in the personal sentiment scrawled in the blank spaces.

With sympathy. Condolences. Great guy will be missed!

Who puts an exclamation mark on a sympathy card?

The same story appeared over and over in the cards from Andrew's closest friends, how he had actually lost his shirt during a day at Ayr Races. It would have been sweet, had Andrew not always insisted that it wasn't him to whom this calamity had befallen. 'There was some boy,' he had explained, 'called Andrew as well, that's where the confusion arose. Maybe someone's cousin; a hanger-on of some sort.' They used it, though, whenever they wanted to bring him down a peg or two. *It's all very well that you floated your company, but we remember when you lost your shirt.*

Some of the handwriting was harder to decipher than others. Some only possible through deduction and elimination – that looked like a J at the start of one name, and a D for the next – must be James and Doreen.

Marissa and Dawn's friends wrote in infantilised writing, not understanding the etiquette of not pouring out their own feelings to the bereaved. It was not just like *when their cat died*, or *when Matthew died in Downton*.

I hoped David's friends had the courtesy of expressing their sympathy to him, since they had by-passed the widow. I supposed they were as single and as clueless as my own son, but without the guidance I provided.

The cards yielded no clues as to the identity of Celia. No wives, no colleagues, no mysterious women only signing their initial. I piled the cards back into their box and stored it away again, then I pulled out a photo album. I didn't know if I should start with the most recent or from way back, so worked randomly. It took a few days, working through the albums, then the packets of prints which had never made it in them. I even turned on Andrew's computer, which I had somehow fallen heir to, and trawled through a vast number of images. Hundreds of the children; thousands of Marissa's two boys, and dozens and dozens of supposedly interesting, what did he call it? Street furniture: bins and lamp-posts, bollards and memorial cobbles. But nothing, not one thing to lead her to Celia.

'So,' David said the next time he deigned to visit. 'Celia.'

'I don't think you need to worry about that. It must just be a coincidence – two people with the same name who died on the same day. It's not that uncommon a name after all.'

But David shook his head and leant across the table in the Quiet Room to take my hand. 'I know who she is, Mum.'

I pulled back. I didn't need to be comforted like a hysteric.

'Mum.' He put on a face which mixed concern with contempt. 'She's his daughter. She was at Dad's funeral, I think you might have seen her, but she wasn't quite ready to meet you and we didn't think it was an appropriate time.'

I laughed. Proper guffawing. Andrew didn't have a secret daughter; it just didn't make any sense. But I stopped laughing when a question sprang into my mind. 'How old?' I asked.

'Eighteen.'

I considered the information, trying to calculate the year of her birth, well, not the year, that didn't even require arithmetic, but what stage we were at when she was born.

'Her mother?'

He just looked at me, and then to Gina who seemed to be enjoying all this and I don't know if he was being stupid or obtuse.

'I can't believe you just took some stranger's word for it.' But then David always was so gullible.

He gave a long sigh before going to fill the kettle. 'She looked like him; sounded like Marissa; held herself like Dawn. I didn't need a DNA test. Besides,' he said, talking in that stop-and-start way he has, 'I remembered her.'

'So, what does she want? She must know there's no money.'

David dunked a teabag into one of the mugs of boiling water, then the other, though he knows I like my tea strong. 'She wants to honour Dad, to be part of things.'

'It's been a year, and yet she just turns up now.'

'I told you, she was at the funeral. And she's just turned 18, it gives her more choices in her life.'

'Well, I have never heard of anything so ridiculous.' I pushed my tea away.

'I can't believe you're still claiming not to know about her.'

'I was away 18 years ago.'

'You were in hospital. I remember,' David said. 'You missed my first day at school.'

'It's not to be spoken about.' I said, as I had done a thousand times. 'It has to be put behind us.'

'But we're all adults. Surely it's good to be more open now.'

'Why? I don't see why all this can't be left in the past.'

'Celia doesn't want it kept quiet anymore. She wants to take her place in the family. She's moving back here.'

'She wants to stake a claim, more like.' I reached for the tea again and gave it a reluctant sip. Weak as water, just as I thought. 'Who did you say her mother was?'

'Her mother wasn't well,' Gina butted in, although I don't understand how she can know anything about it. 'She couldn't cope with another baby, and she abandoned her, so they could both be cared for.'

'Dad did all he could, Mum, he looked after her financially, made sure she had everything she needed. She went to live with Aunt Fay in Nottingham.'

This was all so preposterous: a foundling, a rich benefactor, it was like something out of Dickens. A woman locked in an asylum unable to comprehend the demon within her. Determined not to have her. Sectioned.

I was aware that I had started to shake. David was talking very calmly, laying out photos in front of me: Andrew with a baby, David, Marissa and Dawn looking on. Then pictures of a woman holding Celia, as a baby, as a toddler.

But the cries, the incessant cries, the wailing, the tantrums began again in my ears.

'Stop.' I bundled the photos together and thrust them towards David. 'Whatever this nonsense is, I want it to stop. I will not listen to this anymore.'

'That's maybe enough for today,' Gina said.

But I recognise the woman holding the baby, I have watched her age over many years. Yet she's there, young, seemingly happy, almost normal, certainly not the type who would rise from a park bench and casually walk away from the pram parked beside her. I can see her now, reflected in the barred window of this place they call a home, and have a flicker of memory. And the memory is called Celia.

Colette Coen

Aero Theater

Everybody Knew

Everybody knew

Photographs of the missing decorate
The clearing, totems of a killing time

Mass graves in Srebrenica, in living memory
Eight thousand Muslim men butchered
By militias

The leaders, tried later for war crimes, shrugged
So what

Beyond the barriers, slide-smear matches
To next-of-kin, remains recovered
To make a life, its apportionment of closure
To a murderous self-regard

Satellites photographed the Balkan pits, the killers
Working nights with backhoes, bodies
Scattered a hundred miles
In a hundred holes

Everybody knew

The women bury shadows – months later, another match
Another place, DNA for other parts

Families in the clearing, patient for the gift
Of graves with names, asking officials
Have you found my son – I have his picture here

Estill Pollock

We sit on the iron bench in our garden and I pick at a flaking bit of metal, hold it between my fingertips, crumble it.

The night is quiet. After weeks of panic, people fleeing to God knows where, it seems acceptance has finally come.

I can hear drunken singing in the distance, low and sombre, I recognise the tune but cannot place the song.

I smile at Dylan, he takes my hand and we return to our star-gazing, our waiting.

My children are in bed.

I held their hands when it was time for them to go. I made them brush their teeth and wash their faces, watched as their tiny hands cupped the water and brought it clumsily to their mouths. They giggled at each other, they did not fight tonight and Charlie brushed May's hair for her. Although they are twins, born only seconds apart, Charlie has always acted as an older brother, tending to his sister, always asking for cuddles from her. He was a sensitive boy.

I had even managed to get them new pyjamas for tonight, and I washed their favourite bedding.

I sat with one on either side of me. They listened quietly as I read, but at the end May noticed the tears in my eyes.

"Why are you crying, mummy?" she asked.

Charlie realised too and grabbed my arm as if to pull me away from my pain.

I wiped at my eyes, angry that they had seen. "I'm ok, I just love you both so much."

"Don't be sad mummy, we love you too, don't we, May?" Charlie said.

May nodded and wrapped her hands around my neck. I could feel the softness of her cheek against mine. I could smell her, the sweet tang of sweat, the baby shampoo I still used in her hair and I remembered how it used to be, me holding her when she was barely the size of my forearm, feeding her. She cried so much, she still does, all I ever wanted to do was keep her safe.

I buried my head in her tiny shoulder, wrapped my arms around her fragile chest.

I stood with her still in my arms and carried her to bed. I tucked her under the covers, pulled the duvet to her chin and kissed her head.

Then I moved back to my boy, my beautiful boy. He kissed my cheek as I lowered my head to him. All I could think was 'soft', they were so soft, so small and innocent and soft. Goddamn the world for wishing harm upon the soft.

They smiled at me as I turned the lights out and I had to fight not to fall apart.

We have done our best to protect them from all this, from the knowledge. It hasn't been difficult.

Schools closed the day it was announced, as did workplaces, money and education has become meaningless. Most things have become meaningless. I have realised how flimsy this world was, everything we had built and called our society existed on a sheet of glass, now shattered.

The looters took most of the food but we have had enough. I have heard horror stories, but our home life for the last few months has been pleasant.

We stayed at home with the children. We played with them, enjoyed spending time with them. It is strange, only since the announcement have I realised how grown up they are. Such little personalities, they have taught me so much.

I wipe my eyes and Dylan squeezes my hand tighter. A tether.

"I have something for you," he says.

I look at him and he's smiling at me but his eyes aren't, I see such weight in them.

"What?" I ask.

He leans forward and drops his hand below him, I hear the scraping sound of ice against glass. He holds the bottle out to me.

I blink away my tears and take it. It is damp and cold to the touch, I run my fingers over the bubbles of condensation.

It's champagne, I don't recognise the label but I can tell that it's vintage. I can tell that it's expensive.

"Where did you get this?" I ask.

Dylan takes it from me and hands me two crystal glasses. They belonged to my mother, we only use them for special occasions.

"I did some work for a guy, finished building a swimming pool in his garden that the contractors had abandoned after the announcement. I figure he wanted to spend tonight in the water. He lived alone too, I guess I felt sorry for him. But workers are hard to find these days, and giving me money would have been pointless. He had three of these beauties. Said he didn't want to be so drunk tonight that he couldn't enjoy the show, so I took him up on the offer."

As he speaks he uncorks it, and for a moment the night air is filled with the sharp scent. My mouth waters. I hold the glasses while he pours, my hands are steady.

We look at each other.

"To what comes next," Dylan says and I clink my glass against his. Together we take our first sip. It is fizzy, cool, delicious. Neither of us need to say so.

Dylans throat moves as he swallows, I watch the pulse throbbing in his neck, too fast, far too fast.

My Dylan. He's not a perfect man, he has an anger deep in his soul, always has. I have seen it a few times, though he has never hurt me, only himself.

Still, none of that matters now. I love him, he loves me, that is all.

"Come quickly, I am tasting the stars," Dylan says, and I can tell by the way his voice deepens that he is quoting another.

"Who said that?" I ask.

He looks away for a moment, then back to me, his eyebrows knit together as if he is suddenly experiencing a pain in the centre of his head. "I don't remember," he says softly. Then, "There is so much I don't remember."

I think of the song I had heard the drunk chorus singing earlier, the name still escaping me. "It doesn't matter," I say.

Dylan shivers, despite how humid the night air is. I can't bear to see him so vulnerable, I pull him towards me and kiss him, eyes closed, savouring every second of it.

Three months ago I was a normal woman. Well, I shouldn't word it like that, nobody is 'normal' really, that's what the last few months have taught me, but my life, the way I lived it, it was nothing special. I worked a 9-5 for a retail company, I worked on finances, numbers, I had always been good with numbers. I gossiped with the girls at the office, mostly about the guys. I went on nights out with them once a month. Everything was fine. But I was bored.

I blame myself for that, not bored anymore, am I? Silly woman not seeing how lucky I was. How my place in society was clear and secure.

Until society collapsed.

They say we were never meant to know. The person who discovered it told only a few others, a government somewhere found out and took control of the information. World leaders decided that it was better, kinder, to remain silent, to allow us to continue with our lives in ignorance. But information has to be stored, and stored information is vulnerable. A group of hackers found the reports and published them.

At first we were told they were fakes. A new form of terrorism, meant to drive us to violence and panic, but the scientists said otherwise and the evidence was clear as day: the Earth is hurtling towards a huge meteor storm, which in turn is hurtling towards the Earth. They will hit us, and there is nothing we can do about it.

After it was announced everyone tore each-other apart. Panic spread like a disease with no immunity. Riot and terror descended. Shops were looted, people were slaughtered and left in the street. There are no police anymore, like the rest of us, those who enforced the law are now at home, with their families. Imminent doom creates the perfect state of indifference.

This went on for weeks, until it finally stopped. A candle at last blown out. People often tell you of the calm before the storm but rarely of the one after. The world woke up and decided it had had enough, the rioting stopped, everything stopped, the streets were cleared or left, doors closed, people looked in instead of out.

I think it was then that I stopped praying.

The government returned from whatever dark corner they had been hiding in. Our country's leader stood, ashen faced and despondent on every TV, his voice played on every radio as he announced plan Z, a drug that could be mass produced in a limited time and distributed to all. One drop on the tongue would stop the heart, quickly and effectively. After the broadcast we were told that he had taken the drug himself, since then there has been silence.

After I settled the children, Dylan took them their doses.

I couldn't go with him.

When he returned I asked him if they were settled, a question I have asked him almost every night for the past five years, but this time the words tasted of acid.

He nodded once and wiped at his eyes.

We have not spoken about it.

I hope I did the right thing. I hope they forgive me.

I come back to myself and notice Dylan staring at me. "I think I lost you a second there," he says.

"I'm sorry."

"No, no, it's fine. It's all fine." He smiles and I remember, him on our first date, stood on my doorstep, the flowers and chocolates soaked, the rain pouring from his hair and that smile.

I take another sip of the champagne.

Above us the sky is clear and the stars burn ever on, ever indifferent. I take comfort in the thought that when all this is gone, they will remain, watching.

Will they mourn us?

"You know, when I was a kid I used to be terrified of dying," Dylan says softly. "I always thought it would be something terrible, a plane crash or, as I got older, a war. I heard so much about the ozone layer, I worried about global warming…" his voice trails off. "I guess that I'm just glad that's it's not our fault."

I smile. "Could have waited another hundred years though couldn't it?"

Dylan laughs. "That would have been nice."

We fall into silence again, and again our eyes drift to the sky.

"Are you cold?" Dylan asks eventually as if we are teenager and he is looking for an excuse to lend me his coat.

"I'm fine," I say.

"Yes. Me too."

There is a flash of orange and the sky becomes littered with a thousand burning lights. They tumble toward us, fall like rain.

On instinct I move, my body wanting to find my children, hold them, keep them safe, but they are safe already.

As I look up, a part of me wonders whether we made the right decision. I imagine them, sat at either side of me, their heads turned upwards, I

Dream Catcher 45

imagine their awe, how they wouldn't quite know whether to be amazed or afraid. I would take their hands, tell them that nothing could hurt them, they would laugh, nervously.

"It's beautiful," I say.

Dylan wraps his arm around my shoulder, pulls me close to him, our bodies together.

I hear an explosion, flames rise like an ocean.

I look away, embrace Dylan completely. I hear our glasses fall and smash against the patio, I bury my head in his neck, where I had seen his pulse.

"I love you," he whispers.

I run my fingers through his hair.

I feel him brace.

Mia Lofthouse

1965 Chrysler

REVIEWS

Also received but not reviewed this time were *You're not Dying*, by Kathrin Schmidt, translated by Christina Les; Alison Binney *Other Women's Kitchens*, Clive Donovan *The Taste of Glass*, George Jowett *The Gypsy and the Candy Floss Queen*, Estil Pollock, *One Hundred Poems to Save the World* edited by Zoe Brigley and Kristian Evans, and *Ghosts behind the Door*, by Mig Holder and Tim Dowley. You are welcome to send copies of books you would like reviewed to me at 109 Wensley Drive, Leeds LS7 2LU (the address for all submissions); please be aware we receive more than twice as many review copies as we can place each issue.

Enchanter's Nightshade
by Simon Currie
Yaffle Press, 2020
ISBN 978-1-913122-15-7 pp 79 £10.00

This collection – another excellent production from the relatively new Yaffle press – allows Simon Currie to range far and wide in place and time. Not quite a self-eulogy, the book is rooted in recollection and remembrance and the diverse subject-matter demonstrates clearly the ability of poetry to encompass almost anything – from childhood poo in Headingley to landscapes and galleries in exotic locations across the world. In 'Slipping Free,' a poem dedicated to the Belfast poet Ciaran Carson, Currie explores his approach to poetry in seeking to make poems '…weigh every word / yet court the unknown to stumble on surprise.' At their best these poems of reminiscence and response to place or painting are precise in their narrative and, where the ordinary is transformed by the poet's gaze and skill, into the extraordinary, suitably surprising.

Thus in 'Above Clun' a simple walk, a simple step up a stile stretches his shadow away but suggests more: 'If I step up to reach the top rung, / a shadow head may touch the clouds.' There are poems in this collection which do just that. In particular, Currie is at his most pensive and effective in those poems which embrace the small scale – notably reflections on Headingley where Currie is drawn back into his own and the area's past without sentimentality or romanticism. In '16, Hollin Lane, Headingley' the memories produced by a photo are vivid but the contemporary reality dissociative, 'And can't connect it with our photos.'

'Gardens of Stone,' a simple and touching reflection on the CWGC Stonefall cemetery in Harrogate, honours the war dead with honesty, especially the flyers whose spirits may be still airborne while, in the cemetery, 'men stay, here sixty years / twice their lives.' Currie takes the past on its own terms and doesn't try to extract from his gentle reverie over-weighty philosophical pronouncements. He wears his erudition lightly but can turn the observed moment into something more meaningful.

The marvellous 'Swimming with Sheep' recalls him driving slowly through a herd of sheep making their way up a country lane and, renouncing the Doric shepherd in him, accepting wistfully that, 'me no Lycidas, they'll move off / letting me go on faster, if alone.'

Though there are gems, the least satisfying of the poems are those dealing with the poet's response to places he has travelled to. As Horace wrote *caelum non animum mutant qui trans mare current* and, without that change of the soul the travel poems can become a little too descriptive, too narrative without the sense of the recorded moment having deeper significance for poet and reader. Lawrence Durrell once wrote that 'travel was the best form of introspection,' and this sense of an emerging fruitful dialogue between writer and him/herself to which readers are made party by the writing can allow poems to transcend their exotic singularity. This is a small cavil, though, as more often than not poems are redeemed by a wry humour, a sense of humanity or an exact and surprising image. I have travelled in the Andalusian hills and Currie captures perfectly the view back where, 'the coast beyond is crusted white with resorts.'

A collection well worth a read, not least for Currie's concern for things overlooked and his ability to render them never unimportant.

Patrick Lodge

In Singing, He Composed a Song
by Jeremy Stewart
The University of Calgary Press, 2021
ISBN 9781773852201 pp 80 $16.50

In Singing, He Composed a Song is not an easy read. Written in a variety of poetic styles and illustrated by moody black and white photographs, it explores dark themes: mental ill health, adolescent alienation, suicide, police and institutional brutality, against a background of poverty and bleak urban life. Yet the narrative is compelling and moves to an uplifting ending, celebrating the kindness of friends and the strength of the individual against unfeeling institutions. In singing/living, the musician does indeed create his song.

In many ways this is a novel in verse. It develops quickly, though not necessarily coherently. School and hospital environments are vividly conveyed, as is the harsh Canadian winter. The voices that interrupt fifteen-year-old John Stevenson's narrative, both reflect on and convey his growing confusion and anger. Psychiatric records, transcript of interviews, comments from his friends and adult observers, photographs supposedly taken at the time, all add to the atmosphere. Throughout, there are memorable descriptions and images, as in

> 'Terrible fast clouds
> the sky is never
>
> empty, it is always
> full of sky' ...
> 'DISCHARGE STATUS, alive' ...
> (the 'Silence of an overturned car.')

The book ends with a fine series of couplets. Though apparently random, together they give a sense of resolution:

> 'I'll come home now
> thanks for not hanging up ...
> sun rises and falls and clouds fly
> overhead while I remain.'

The photographs create a sense of immediacy but I'm not sure the reproduction here does them justice. In my copy some seem too dark, especially 'John's band performing at the Legion Hall' which is almost illegible. That's a pity as they give an extra dimension to the narrative.

I thoroughly recommend this book, but would suggest that it needs careful reading to be fully appreciated.

Pauline Kirk

All the Men I Never Married
by Kim Moore
Seren, 2021
ISBN 9781781726419 pp 72 £9.99 AND
What the Trumpet Taught me
by Kim Moore
smith|doorstep, 2022
ISBN 978194914140 pp 144 £8.99

The prolific and multi-talented Kim Moore offers two very different sets of insights in these most recent publications. A professional brass player as well as poet, Moore is frequently heard on BBC broadcasts, is in keen demand to judge major poetry competitions, and (when lockdown permits) is an engaging performer of her own work. She is also co-director of the Kendal Poetry Festival.

All the Men I Never Married is a striking contribution to the #MeToo chorus; the forty-eight poems (titled just by their number) express desire, frustration, rage, disgust, hurt, guilt, and much more. But there is a very distinctive voice here, despite the familiarity of the themes. Moore is by turns incisive, witty and passionate. Her use of both prose poems and lineated verse structures is taut; her endings are strongly focused, and there is memorable choice of phrases; I especially loved the understated image of

> 'the trombonist I went drinking with
> how we lay twice a week in each other's beds
> like two unlit candles.' (1)

There is guilt folded like a handkerchief

> 'so I put it in my pocket
> carry it with me always.' (25)

The penultimate poem in the collection pulls off the palindromic form with a success rarely found. The anaphoric (6) with its repeated 'That' is a lesson in how to offer more than the sum of its parts, a classic example of how tightly Moore controls the endings: given the other string to her bow, it is tempting to use musical terminology here – a crescendo? A tempo change? A variant of *stretto*?

> 'That being our bodies in public is a dangerous thing.
> That being in public is a dangerous thing.
> That our bodies are dangerous things.' (yes!)

The sonnet sequence (31) (written in solidarity with the poet Helen Mort, who was victim to Deep Fake activity) is an especially well-crafted piece; here the picking up of the final line of each of the seven sonnets, and reusing as the first line of the next evokes cleverly the enmeshed entrapment of the individual within the exploitative crime discussed, and depicts on the page how something (in this case, the image of the woman) is distorted and manipulated. Moore's insistence that 'I'm making this a #NotAllMen free zone' will strike a chord with the many women who have experienced sexual assault of all kinds. The rear cover testimonial by Malika Booker praises her 'poetic witnessing'; I can't improve on that as a peon to a serious artist at the peak of her expressive powers.

What the Trumpet Taught Me covers some of the same themes, but with less sex and more music. It is a deliciously pocket sized volume of very short prose pieces (ideal for percussionists to browse in the long bars of rest, perhaps?). Disclosed gradually, intermittently, is a history of Moore's romance and estrangement with the life of a professional brass player, both the putatively glamourous life of playing in gigs, and the harsher realities of teaching and recording.

The men she encounters on this special and temporal journey are objectified with brief monikers – 'The man who dances like Mick Jagger', the recurrent 'man I met in Germany,' who clearly on balance did her no favours. Implicit in this discretion is that she was shaped by these relationships; but that they were perhaps less important than the relationship she has (or had) to her music making, especially her fostering of a love of performance in students in often deprived situations.

References to the music she plays as a trumpet player provide depth and perspective, like a long angle lens pointed towards the stage. After a hiatus of some years, she starts playing in a ten-piece soul band. At this late stage in her performing career (to date!), she learns that 'there's no conductor, nobody to watch, other than the in-breath of the singers, other than the lifting of the sticks by the drummer from the corner of my eye.' The sense of collaboration, collusion created when you make music is so well expressed here, and/but it also mirrors the collaboration of writer and reader.

Compared to *All The Men I Never Married*, there is even more allusiveness, even more restraint from the over-effusive quality of some 'confessional' poetry doing the rounds at present. Her willingness to leave space for her reader to do some of the work, to find their own meaning, makes her work sharp, memorable, engaging. In the middle of a performance of Handel's *Messiah* she learns that a friend she had expected to see in the audience has died in a car crash. Moore's bald statement of how she carried on after the interval, having heard that news, is purely factual: it acts as a metaphor for her life to that point, perhaps: 'If the first part of the *Messiah* concerns itself with redemption, and the second with suffering, the third is all about victory over death.'

The unembroidered statement almost registers bathos; even the paragraph which follows omits any emotional over-sharing, leaving space for the reader to take their own deep breath as they turn the page. It is not for another twenty pages that she cites (*vis a vis* a memorial performance for victims of a mass shooting in St Bees) the terribly, beautifully, poignant words that accompany the trumpet part in that final section of Messiah: 'Behold, I show you a mystery. /We shall not all sleep, but we shall all be changed./In a moment, in the twinkling of an eye/ at the last trumpet.'

Play it again, Kim.

Hannah Stone

Hate Story
by Jeff Cottrill
Dragonfly Publishing, 2022
ISBN: 9 780645 350565 pp323   £9.52

Jeff Cottrill's novel *Hate Story* brings to mind Wilkie Collins's recipe of 'the influence of character on circumstances.' The novel is a sustained satirical study of the unpoliced flourishing of online trolling and its devastating effect on those targeted. The characters that influence these uniquely twenty-first-century circumstances are convincingly drawn, their outcome matters to us, and the tone ranges from detached mockery to macabre farce. The novel opens with mock-documentary coverage of a vandalised funeral, and continues in the form of investigative journalism to uncover the extent to which the corpse had been a creep or not. But this is not a novel of comfortable binaries. It is an examination of thoughtless groupthink in the pursuit of power and a twisted kind of belonging: 'Another anonymous witness, asked why he hated Shoreditch so much, responded, "Because he's a scumbag! That's what everyone says."' Even the protagonist is guilty of chasing the thrill of lobbing linguistic grenades into the melee.

The motivation of trolls has been explored by others, including John Ronson and Mary Beard – Beard resolves her experience of trolling by talking about it to her thousands of followers, as well as meeting and befriending the trolls – a dual approach that has worked well. Then again, there's the knotty issue of freedom of speech, and of the good that can be done by online people power; Fichman and Sanfilipo, in *Under the Cyber Bridge*, talk about 'justifiable trolling for ideological purposes'.

But even John Stuart Mill, advocate of freedom of expression, drew the line at 'a positive instigation to some mischievous act,' and it is this line that Cottrill examines, not least through the development of his very likable, energetic but flawed protagonist, Jackie. It's only as she uncovers more and more about the hunted Shoreditch that she begins to examine her own behaviour and to be haunted by terrible guilt over the potential repercussions of her own actions – in short, she begins to *think*. In a world of cyberbullying and cancel culture, where we are constantly navigating a dystopian, virtual, post-truth world dominated by rumour and cries of 'fake news' on every side, where anyone can hide behind the anonymity of multiple online avatars, how far can any of us really stand back, not get involved, or even truly avoid taking part? Where our heroine is culpable too, how far is too far?

Amina Alyal

One Language
by Anastasia Taylor-Lind
smith|doorstep, 2022
ISBN 9781914914102 pp62   £10.99

One of the features which drew me to *Dream Catcher* as a reader, submitter and now editor was its showcasing of original art work. I have a soft spot for poetry books which include art work of any form, be it line drawings (favourite examples are Alice Oswald's *Weeds and Wild Flowers*, and the poignantly almost-post mortem *Sorry about the Mess* by Heather Trickey, whose daughter Silva Brindle provided the whimsical inside/outside cover illustrations), paintings or photographs (in which field our occasional reviewer Nick Allen is an expert practitioner.) Taylor-Lind's book, the winner of the International Book and Pamphlet Competition run by the Poetry Business, goes beyond offering illustrations as an adjunct to the poetry; they are part of its 'language.'

In *One Language*, the photos are an integral part of the work, created by an artist who is a photo-journalist as much as she is a poet. The 'language' employed in this work is thus complex, multi-layered, alarming and unavoidable; driving its way straight to the nub of the matter despite literal and metaphorical roadblocks, political and historical ignorance on the part of the reader, and all the other baggage that readers bring to a work of art.

You can start by 'reading' the cover images, which include the heart-breaking witness to the evacuation of the Dadivank Monastery during the Armenian civil war (when this part of Nagorno-Karabakh was allocated a fresh identity which put it inside a 97% majority Muslim zone), or the inside front cover with its images of female teams conducting door-to-door polio vaccinations in Afghanistan in 2013 – with each of the medical professionals swathed from head to foot in blue burkas, which causes them to look like ectopic images of the Virgin Mary, escaped from renaissance paintings. A diverse set of single, intimate images are carefully inter-leaved through the rest of the book.

The writings themselves offer an appalling and necessary commentary on life and death in war zones. The 'Field notes' evoking the Dadivank event (at the height of the pandemic) are identified by precise times: 9.05, 11.36, 14.15 … each poem is accompanied by said 'field notes' capturing the experience of 'the only journalists wearing facemasks and the only all-female reporting team.' These remind me of the vignettes from Radio 4's 'From our Own Correspondent', which features footage from embedded journalists in global places of interest (to put it euphemistically). But there is plenty of poetry here, too –

'Chainsaws murmur and woodcutter's flashlights
are constellations of fireflies on the dark hillside
as Armenians loot the land for winter wood.' (18.10)

Poems recording treatment of the injured in field hospitals unpin poetic insights with filmic quality – though the refrain 'CUT' in 'Al Hikma Hospital' surely refers to not just the shift of camera angle but the cutting open of clothes and bodies to remove shrapnel and bullets, the hands 'stitching something together in a big red hole.' That these atrocities continue on a daily basis is brought home by poems from Donetsk, written before the current invasion of Ukraine. And the gentler mundane realities of human experience emerge tentatively at times.

The section 'Stories No One Wants to Hear' is closer to home, showing Taylor-Lind's ability to explore her own family history, but also returns us to the war zone. It is here that we read the phrase '*Anastasia, some people only understand one language*' and are forced to confront the place of physical violence in communication, and the fact that 'Pacifism is a privilege of the peaceful and empowered – inside the home, in our communities and on a global scale.' Reading this as a proto-Quaker, I found this to be a very necessary challenge.

A brilliant, disturbing book which forces you to re-evaluate many of your preconceptions, your own understanding of the power and potential for truth *and* corruption that language can provide.

Hannah Stone

The Underlook
by Helen Seymour
smith|doorstop, 2022
ISBN 978-1-914914-00-3 pp 63 £10.99

One trend in the academic writing on the psychology of disability is to shift the focus from the impact of any 'impairments' upon the individual towards the way that the 'disabled' actually make sense of and deal with the external social and physical environments which ignores, marginalises and actually *disables* an individual. Helen Seymour, who self-identifies as a disabled writer, is plain in this collection about what she has faced. The book's cover blurb is unambiguous in noting what you can expect in this collection which is informed by 'experiences of physical disability, surgery and medical trauma.' Not immediately a bag of laughs – though Seymour's humour is at times dark, visceral and outrageously funny – but it is undoubtedly a bag of exceptional poetry which, while never polemical, is explicit about the experiences she has had.

More importantly the collection goes well beyond the individual's health issues and deals brilliantly with the disabling environment in which she has had to operate. To 'underlook' is to miss or omit something because one has looked too low – a perfect image to express the way in which disabled people are often rendered invisible and mute or subject to processes which can seem, from a squint perspective, surreal and crazy. Seymour's poetry does not let this happen. It is good that her voice as a disabled writer is heard but, in the sense that she is a poet of acute perception and talent, the label may well be seen to limit here.

The collection is introduced with an epigraph from Matthew Holness whose short story 'Possum' – from which the quote used derives – was made into a deeply disturbing and challenging film. Holness once wrote that he felt it was important not to give the audience any safety nets 'to feel like they knew where they were.' Seymour seems to have taken this to heart. At her best the poems subvert expectation and draw the reader into a distorted and surreal world that, in evidence of Seymour's craft, almost seems real. Poems like 'Crack' or 'Beep' offer a perspective on medical processes in marvellously fractured narratives. Here heroines are

'...found wandering around the fracture clinic
falling in love with broken people.' ('Crack')

or admitting

> 'Everytime I see you I vomit.'

Here are pleas to be recognised, to be seen for what you are – not made invisible, even from the best possible motives;

> 'I wasn't even a woman, but some animal
> you were fond of.'

Even caring is only another means of ignoring the person,

> …you looked
> at me like I was trapped in a snare,
> whispering, 'hey there lil' bunny…
> let's get you cleaned up and on your way home.' ('Heaving').

The collection is formidable in suggesting a person semi-trapped by a disability and lacking agency in a potentially violent and unpredictable world of the normal (for everyone else). It is Seymour's poetic craft, wit and powerful imagery – as well as her refusal to take it – which makes this book spark with life. The invitation at the end of 'Falling' to see irony in the claim of

> 'the limpness, the privilege
> to inhabit such blatant living dud,'

should be rejected. In this collection Seymour gives no apologies for who she is and it is a privilege to be Helen Seymour who, as a poet, is much more than the issues of disability she deftly and brutally dissects.

Patrick Lodge

The Thoughts
by Sarah Barnsley
smith|doorstop, 2022
ISBN 978-1-914914-02-7 pp95 £10.99

The Thoughts by Sarah Barnsley is a thoughtful, unflinching and often humorous look at the turmoil of obsessive-compulsive disorder. Sarah explores the cyclical and torturous pattern of intrusive thoughts, and their resultant compulsions. In reading these poems we are taken into the mind of an OCD sufferer and shown the mundane world in a new and disturbing light. We follow the persona as they obsessively check their emails out of fear that they may have revealed their deepest secrets to everyone they know, and we feel their dread as thoughts begin to spiral at a train station.

There is humour to be found in these works too, such as the poem 'System Administrator', that playfully make fun of the persona's own experience with intrusive thoughts and ruminations. This poem as well as many others, such as 'Prefrontal Cortex' and 'We have made a Number of Key Appointments,' act to personify the obsessive thoughts to something outside of oneself, which is often a helpful way of looking at mental illness. However, underneath the layers of humour and extended metaphors there is a real and often harrowing tale of how debilitating this condition is; at times poems become hard to read, taking on the form of checkerboards or magazine articles. Other times the reader has to turn the book, or read sideways, in order to understand the words. This creates a kind of chaos and uncertainty on the page that reflects the mind of the persona.

A necessary and important work, that opened my eyes to the reality of obsessive-compulsive disorder.

Mia Lofthouse

Offcumdens
by Bob Hamilton and Emma Storr
Fair Acre Press, 2022
ISBN 978 1 911048671 pp 108   £19.99

Offcumdens is a gloriously full-hearted collaboration, with a real symbiosis between image and verse. As Philip Gross writes in his endorsement, 'Each double page is a conversation.' Storr's work may well already be known to readers –through her elegant pamphlet *Heart Murmer* (Calder Valley Press, 2019); this collaboration with photographer Bob Hamilton captures Yorkshire so genuinely that it is hard to credit they are both (like your editor) an 'offcumden', meaning an incomer to the area.

Although the front cover might suggest a focus on landscape, between the covers we find a myriad of Yorkshire personas, human and canine, alongside urban vignettes and traditional dales landscapes. Familiar though the scenes may be to devotees of this landscape, the messages from these pairings is never predictable. The photos, like the poems, 'tell it slant', for example 'Cycle' shows part of a wheel and a leg, taken from above and the bizarrely deconstructed reflection of it (a sunny dale in the dales – who'd have thought?). I especially enjoyed the photos where the yoking of sunlight and cloud are at their most weird – how opportune to capture a 'Brocken Spectre,' though as Storr remind us, waiting for the perfect image can involve much chilly hanging around.

'Look at me.
Not my image.
I'm here. Freezing.' ('Walking Away').

The poems themselves bounce ideas off the images, so the spooky view from inside Gaping Gill ('Harness') sparks a thoughtful poem about parental 'letting go.' Here, as so often, there is real tenderness, as a foil to the wit and lightness of touch found in other poems.

The dialogue is continued in the notes at the back of the book, where both poet and artist give their notes on the genesis of the pairings. Here there is an almost scholarly attention to detail, even when it records the serendipitous nature of the creative output. This is a rare example of a really covetable 'coffee table' book (do people still have coffee tables?) to dip into for either visual or verbal nourishment.

Hannah Stone

Index of Authors

Alan Gillott 5, 26, 27
Amina Alyal 10, 11, 93
Chris Scriven 49
Ciaran Buckley 75
Ciáran Dermott 39
Clifford Liles 55
Clint Wastling 24, 25
Clive Donovan 38
Colette Coen 77
Daniel Nemo 60
David Harmer 44
David J Costello 40
David Sapp 57
Delilah Heaton 32
Doreen Hinchliffe 45
Emily Zobel Marshall 53
Estill Pollock 82
Fionola Scott 47
Greg McGee 1
Hannah Stone 3, 8, 9, 91, 94, 98
Helen Heery 48
James B. Nicola 69
Jo Haslam 58
Joe Williams 12, 13
John Gilham 14, 15
Julian Matthews 43

Justin Lloyde 68
Kathleen Strafford 30
Kieran Furey 42
Lance Nizami 56
Mark Pearce 70
Martha Glaser 61
Martin Reed 50
Mary Michaels 74
Mia Lofthouse 83, 97
Michael Henry 72
Michael Newman 73
Miriam Sulhunt 35
Oz Hardwick 31
Pat Simmons 46
Patrick Lodge 89, 96
Pauline Kirk 20, 21, 90
Peter Datyner 33
Rose Drew 16, 19
Simon Tindal 52
Stephanie Conybeare 37
Stephen Capus 34
Susie Williamson 17
Tanya Parker 22, 23
Timothy Houghton 59
Tracy Dawson 51
Wilf Deckner 65

Dream Catcher 45

Other anthologies and collections available from Stairwell Books

Title	Author
Fatherhood	CS Fuqua
Herdsmenization	Ngozi Olivia Osuoha
On the Other Side of the Beach, Light	Daniel Skyle
Words from a Distance	Ed. Amina Alyal, Judi Sissons
All My Hands Are Now Empty	Linda Baker
Fractured	Shannon O'Neill
Unknown	Anna Rose James, Elizabeth Chadwick Pywell
When We Wake We Think We're Whalers from Eden	Bob Beagrie
Awakening	Richard Harries
Geography Is Irrelevant	Ed. Rose Drew, Amina Alyal, Raef Boylan
Starspin	Graehame Barrasford Young
Out of the Dreaming Dark	Mary Callan
A Stray Dog, Following	Greg Quiery
Blue Saxophone	Rosemary Palmeira
Steel Tipped Snowflakes 1	Izzy Rhiannon Jones, Becca Miles, Laura Voivodeship
Where the Hares Are	John Gilham
Something I Need to Tell You	William Thirsk-Gaskill
The Glass King	Gary Allen
The River Was a God	David Lee Morgan
A Thing of Beauty Is a Joy Forever	Don Walls
Gooseberries	Val Horner
Poetry for the Newly Single 40 Something	Maria Stephenson
Northern Lights	Harry Gallagher
Nothing Is Meant to be Broken	Mark Connors
Heading for the Hills	Gillian Byrom-Smith
More Exhibitionism	Ed. Glen Taylor
Rhinoceros	Daniel Richardson
The Beggars of York	Don Walls
Lodestone	Hannah Stone
Unsettled Accounts	Tony Lucas
Learning to Breathe	John Gilham
New Crops from Old Fields	Ed. Oz Hardwick
The Ordinariness of Parrots	Amina Alyal
Homeless	Ed. Ross Raisin
Somewhere Else	Don Walls
Taking the Long Way Home	Steve Nash

For further information please contact rose@stairwellbooks.com

www.stairwellbooks.co.uk
@stairwellbooks